# A MERE FARMBOY

Edmund Edward Austin

**CeeTeC Publishing**
**Abbotsford, Canada**

The author expresses heartfelt thanks to Art Heming who designed and implemented the cover layouts. Similarly, the same to Dr. L.T. Holdcroft for his counsel, advice and help in the preparation of the manuscript for this publication. The author has appreciative memories of having Dr. Holdcroft as his teacher during his studies at Western Bible College, Winnipeg, Manitoba.

### A MERE FARMBOY

### ISBN 0-9733753-6-1

**Library of Congress Cataloging-in-Publication Data**

Austin, E.E. (Edmund Edward),
   A mere farmboy / Edmund Edward Austin
   p.cm.
   Autobiography
   ISBN 0-9733763-6-1 (pbk.)

   1. Austin, E.E. (Edmund Edward), 1925- 2. Pentecostal Assemblies of Canada–Clergy–Biography. 3.Clergy–Canada–Biography.

BX8762.Z8A935 2006          289.9

Printed in Canada

PUBLISHED BY

| CeeTeC | U.S. Address: |
|---|---|
| PO Box 466 | PO Box 1117 |
| Abbotsford BC  V2T 6Z7 | Sumas WA 98295 |

☎(604) 853-5352  or  (604) 807-5831

# THE JOURNEY ROADMAP

*To my wife, Grace*
*and*
*Daughters Cheryl and Charlene,*
*Son-in-Law Mark*
*And*
*Grandson Aaron Edward*
*who have*
*filled my life with joy.*

6

# Acknowledgements

In one's lifetime many people influence its course and activity. In no less fashion was my life shaped in one way or another. Persons with whom I associated in personal administrative and ministry service, made my life so abounding. Losing my father at eleven years of age, my mother imparted to me love, discipline, and challenging strength. For this and many other reasons, I will ever be grateful as I live in the memories of her beautiful life.

Throughout my years of ministry, I appreciated the fellowship of the Pentecostal Assemblies of Canada. There was always a sense and warmth of belonging to a structured Christian Fellowship of men and women of like faith, founded and grounded upon the Holy Scriptures.

We were a part of ministers, missionaries, evangelists and executives whose ministry was the vital part of our own desire to share the gospel with the world.

It was my honor to serve this fellowship as a pastor, educator and servant of that host of church members. From the start, I was involved with Executive service as well as pastoral ministry. It included District Christ's Ambassadors Executive, College Faculty, District Assistant Superintendent in Manitoba and British Columbia, Presbyter in Ontario, three Bible College boards and many national committees.

I thank God for the heritage of godly leaders before me and the host of fellow credential holders with whom I served. We saw the work of God prosper and rejoiced together to see God glorified in our combined efforts. To God be the Glory Forever!

I wish to express my appreciation to my family in the assistance in typing the biography. From my wife's father, even though I never knew him, yet from his art and his Bible notes I gleaned an inspiration of a model of someone whose writings revealed a profound knowledge of the Bible and artistic talent.

Also, I wish to give special thanks to published author [*The Eternal Purpose of God* and *A New Heaven and a New Earth*] and writer of many essays, Walter Rachinski, for his counsel and extensive editorial assistance in the writing of my life's journey as well as writing the Foreword. We will always cherish the friendship of Walter and Ollie. They are precious people.

In this biography I will name many people with whom I was associated and which will always remain in my memory. Many have passed on and others still remain. I wish to pay tribute to all of them and value the honor and privilege I had to share life with them. We shared some of the most exciting times and I was honored to be their pastor and friend.

# Foreword

In one of my books we wrote that, from an evangelical perspective, one might think all men called by God to a high profile ministry, would have been brought up in an intensely spiritual environment.

Our expectation of it may be conditioned by how Noah was pressed into service. We see it again in the call of Samuel, and later, in the anointing of David, as the second king in the newly formed monarchical reign over the nation of Israel. But God, who knows the end from the beginning in the lives of those he calls, shows us that he is not bound to stereotype.

The early church, when they heard of Paul's conversion and call to ministry, probably thought—Go Figure! Why would God call such an evil man who led a major persecution against the early Christians, to become perhaps one of the most theologically profound Apostles, on which, together with the other apostles and prophets, was to be laid the foundation of the Christian Church.

No matter what our origins or family history might be, what we do see in Scripture is, God starts all of us on the same plateau. It is as the message given to Zechariah (4:10) "Who despises the day of small things?" Israel would learn to rejoice when they saw the plumb line in Zerubbabel's hand to complete the task of rebuilding the temple in Jerusalem. So it is of all God's servants, who receive the message: "Not by might nor by power, but by my Spirit," says the Lord Almighty (4:6).

This is precisely the acknowledgement of Ed Austin, whom the Lord privileged me to become acquainted with. Having the opportunity to gain a little insight of Ed Austin's beginnings, yet not having come to know him as a colleague in the ministry of God's kingdom until very recently, has been a rewarding experience for me. Both Ed and Grace are saintly people, with a dimension of ministry not commonly paralleled.

Secrets to success are not mysteriously hidden in the folds of divine revelation. Repeatedly, in the lives of God's servants, whether in the Old Testament or New Testament, the standard for success in the ministry, regardless of what title or position of leadership, has always been openly disclosed in Scripture. One that applies to all of God's children is the promise: You will seek me and find me when you seek me with all your heart (Jeremiah 29:13).

Ed, in his biography, stated: "It never ceases to amaze me that God would choose me as one of his servants in gospel ministry to the degree it brought me into contact with a host of people into whose life I was privileged to contribute a spiritual dimension." But it is within the tapestry of these very words that "greatness" is woven into the very fabric of his ministry. What remains to be defined is what is a high profile ministry?

For all those who have known Ed over a long period of time, as I have just recently been privileged to get to know him, there would be certainty over a common agreement in the life and ministry of Ed Austin. And what might that common agreement represent?

Unquestionably, Ed Austin took seriously the words of our Lord, to settle an argument started among the disciples, concerning greatness. Jesus gave them this conclusion: "For he who is least among you all—he is greatest" (Luke 9:48). The history of Ed's ministry emulates both this and the spirit of the apostle Paul, who said: "...I have made myself servant unto all..." (1 Corinthians 9:19).

Ed is in the company of giant killers. David, the youngest of Jesse's eight sons, was God's choice as the next king of Israel after the rejection of Saul. Ed, the youngest in his parent's family of sons, was singled out by the hand of God, to receive a shepherd's heart and instill a spiritual dimension of God's message of love through repentance and the forgiveness of sins.

Every reader of this biography will be blessed with the realization that, insofar as God is no respecter of persons, those who follow in Ed's footsteps and emulate his servant heart will also reach the biblical threshold of greatness!

*Walter Rachinski*
**Author, *The Eternal Purpose of God* &**
***A New Heaven and a New Earth***

# Introduction

In May 1996, I experienced the loss of my last brother Mike. It was then that the realization came to me rather forcefully I was the only one left in my immediate family. The future not being what it used to be, the inclination to write a family history, and record for my own children, happenings in my life beyond the reach of their own memory, pressed itself into my consciousness.

Memory is the most precious gift God has given to us. But even God provided a written record for his family, to tell us all he wanted us to know about him. So, I felt the need to leave for my family a record of my life as well as our lives together as a family, which would include more than they themselves were a part of during their growing up years.

What may be contained in this biography may or may not be of much interest to family outsiders. On the other hand, it may inspire others in understanding that, personal tidbits represent moments of cherished memories worth recording.

In retrospect, all that has been experienced in my life, were not merely happenstance occurrences. An overwhelming sense of gratitude fills my heart in the realization that what could have been simple obscurity, by God's grace and guiding hand, the Lord led me into a life of Gospel ministry.

I did not rise to newspaper fame, nor did God lead me into some BIG-BUDGET ministry as appears to be essential to achieve a high level of prominence and international recognition. Also, my circle of Christian ministry was to me more fulfilling than any secular fame this world could have offered me.

It never ceases to amaze me that God would choose me as one of his servants in gospel ministry to the degree it brought me into contact with a host of people into whose life I was privileged to contribute a spiritual dimension. You see, God is in the people business. So, the privilege to work in his kingdom in this people business, has brought a mountain of experiences. Every one of them is cherished.

No servant engages in self-boasting. Everything then to be made note of as one of the Lord's servants, is because of what the Lord has allowed me to be a part of and enjoy.

It is then because of my wife, Grace, and my daughters, Cheryl and Charlene, I give thanks to God. The summary of my life is provided so that you can reflect on the privilege given me to be a faithful husband, father, and a ministry servant of God.

God bless you. I love you.

# Chapter 1

## *In the Beginning*

I was born on what is usually the hottest day of the year in the prairies. The big event happened on July 31, 1925 in a farmhouse just a couple of miles north of Angusville, Manitoba.

The farm was known as the "Brunt" place. The house was a two-story frame building, just a few hundred feet from the road. It must not have had any value after having served as the berthing of one E. E. Austin.

I was there on the occasion of it being burned to the ground. The occasion was a "potato digging" bee with some relatives. My mother was making dinner for the gang. It seemed she stoked the kitchen stove with too much fire while she was cooking. The pipes, which went up through the upper floor to the chimney, over- heated and the house caught on fire. I recall mother being upstairs during the inflamed upper part, trying to salvage whatever she could throw out the window. Someone frantically called her to "get out of there." Thankfully, she reached safety, but most of our belongings were lost.

I also remember my cousin and I (probably three years of age) watching things being dragged out of the main floor. In particular, mom had been frying eggs for dinner and as they were carried out, half-fried eggs were scattered over the ground, which struck my cousin and me as kind of funny. We laughed while crying at the same time.

Talk about house fires! My mother told me that during their homesteading days in northern Manitoba, they suffered another house fire. This was a log house they built and apparently, during the night as they slept, the house caught on fire.

Mother awakened father from a deep sleep, calling him to get my two older brothers, who were then around five and six years old, out of the house. My mother said, she called out "The house is on fire."

Dad awoke dazed and grabbed a cup sitting on a table beside the bed and threw it right through the window. Gaining his composure, he proceeded to evacuate family and belongings.

With our "burned" house gone, the family moved a few miles away to an empty house called the "Huston" place. The original homestead with barn and buildings, however, was retained by the family. My brothers worked the land and raised cattle and other stock. We only lived in the Huston house for a short period and then moved on to another farm that belonged to a store owner by the name of Mr. Waldman. Our house was a log house and we always referred to it as the "Jews Place." The family worked both quarter sections of the land. I remember that behind the log house there were great patches of wild strawberries, which we would go and pick for our desserts.

I do not remember too much of the events that took place, outside of the routine chores and my playing in the yard. One incident I do recall was mother trying to give me the strap while I crouched under the dining room table. The punishment was because I was afraid to go upstairs when told to go to bed.

It was from here that I started school. I went with my brothers and sister into Angusville. In grade one, my first teacher's name was Miss Clarke. I must have done exceptionally well, because I was moved up to grade two half way through the term, and my teacher's name, for the rest of grade two, as well as grade three, was Miss Gertrude Staples. She was the daughter of the railroad station master.

We walked to school during the summer time and traveled by horse and cutter in wintertime. It was on one of those journeys home after school, when my sister decided to run along side the cutter. The result was, she contracted triple pneumonia, which almost took her life. I will tell you more about it later.

One oft repeated event on the farm was the swimming on the farm lake. We always had a gang of people who would gather on Sunday afternoon for a swim. Many happy incidents took place and friendships were formed.

We lived on the Waldman farm only a short time, until my brothers, Mike and Carl, decided to rent land in Russell. My brother Frank and my father would go to Detroit during the long winter and work in the Ford car factory. When we moved to Russell, dad decided to build a small house on our homestead and not go to Russell.

I might mention that, the relationship between my parents was very strained and I don't know under what circumstances they parted. But it never took the route of legal separation of divorce. It was when my dad was building this house that he took ill, which ultimately took his life. More on this later.

I recall the great move to Russell. We rented the "Matheson" farm. With three wagon loads, we journeyed the 14 miles to our new place. This was the farthest from home I had ever been. Here I was, at age seven, driving a team with a wagon, hayrack, and some hay upon which was placed our family organ. Attached were horses and cows, followed by some free-running stock.

To conclude my memories of Angusville, I recall going to town with my family. In those days, the town was vibrant with many stores, cafes and Saturday night was bustling with all the families coming in to shop, visit, and talk shop.

The mode of transportation was horse and buggy in the summer—horse and cutter in the winter. Whenever we went visiting in the winter, I remember mother had a foot warmer, which was filled with hot coals to keep our feet warm. We also had heavy blankets and skin hides to keep out the cold.

Although I don't recall going, the community talked about "Fish Lake" north of town about 10-12 miles where everyone went fishing for "jack fish."

Our many neighbors were close by and we would visit back and forth as that was our social life.

One family by the name of "Kodloski" lived just a quarter of a mile from our place (my birthplace). Their family was made up of father Mike, mother Nettie, Grandma, probably

80 years of age, with three daughters—Rose, Mary and Annie—and two sons—Dan and Frank. They were older than I, but my brother Dan would take me along for the visits.

I mention this, for it was on the occasion of one of these visits that on our return home, my brother was pulling me on a sled across a frozen lake, across which was hanging a wire. Without thinking, he threw the wire over his head and proceeded onward, forgetting I was behind and my head was just at wire height. The result was, I got a cut just under my eye, which fortunately missed my eye. If it had not, it would have been disastrous. Arriving home with blood all over, my mother doctored me up, after which she gave Danny a hefty scolding for his carelessness.

Some other events of that time included my cousin Carl being shot and killed over some trapping dispute. Also, a man in the community who was having an affair with the wife of another man, resulted in the birth of quintuplets. He decided to kill all five and ended up being charged with murder and was hung at the Headingly jail near Winnipeg. Yet another incident was when one neighbor had purchased an old Model T Ford and was taking his father for a ride. Apparently, they were going a little too fast, missing a turn and scaring dear dad, who hollered, "Hold her Newt, she's heading for the rhubarb."

Leaving for Russell, a disconnection from most of the relatives who remained in and around Angusville, resulted. Being the youngest of the family, I can only list to the best of my memory some of the family history, which I will do in the next chapter.

# Chapter 2

## *Family History*

I never knew my grandparents for they had passed away before I was born. On my mother's side, her parents came to Canada from Poland when she was ten years of age. She was the only girl. Named Magdalena, she was always called "Lena". Her two brother siblings were named Mike and John.

I do not know when my father and his parents came to Canada, but I would assume about the same time as did my mother's parents. My father, whose name was Kost, was the only son. He had two sisters, whose names were Annie and Winnie. I do not really know on what side of mother's parents there was a death, but I think her father was widowed, by whom he had a daughter. Mother always spoke of her half-sister by the name of Donya.

I shall list the members of each family, so that at least we can count the number of cousins. But first, I want to tell you that there was a sister and brother marriage relationship, which made my circle of aunts and uncles smaller. I am told that my Uncle John wanted to marry my dad's sister Winnie. She would consent only if Uncle John's sister (my mother) married Aunt Winnie's brother Kost (my father). Well, as it went, both marriages took place. It probably was the reason that my parents parted as I indicated in the previous chapter.

The families include: Uncle John (he was always referred to as JW. Why? I don't know) and Aunt Winnie's children were: Carrie, Louis, Carl, Minnie, and Julia. At this writing, Carrie, Minnie and Julia (Judy) are still living. Louis went to the United States. I do not know whether he is still alive. Carl was killed in the shooting accident. Aunt Winnie lived into her nineties.

Uncle Mike and wife (can't remember her name) had Edgar, Lyle, Rose, Mary, Bert and Philip. I don't know if any of these are still alive.

Uncle Tony and Aunt Annie (she was my dad's sister) had Frank, Tom, Minnie, John, Adolph and Vera. All are deceased.

Dad and mother had Mike (who died at 2 years of age due to pneumonia), Frank, Mike, Carl, Helen, Danny and Edmund. Yours truly is the only surviving member of the family.

The following is the history of my immediate family. As I indicated in the previous chapter, we moved to Russell in the summer of 1933. We located on the Matheson Farm, one mile west of the town of Russell.

By this time, Frank and Mike were out of school, as it was necessary for them to work on the farm. I believe they only went to grade eight. Carl, Helen, Danny and I attended Russell Collegiate.

Carl was born in Angusville in 1915. Mother was very insistent that Carl get his education because of his hand with which he was born. She felt he should follow some vocation, which would not necessitate manual labor. The hand had only two fingers and was smaller than ordinary. His arm, however, was as normal as the other. He could make me yelp if I had my wrist between those two fingers. He did complete his grade eleven.

Carl always felt very conscious of that hand. As it turned out, he never went into any business vocation, but became our wealthiest farmer. He farmed west of Russell growing grain. He also had over 100 head of purebred Hereford cattle. He retired and lived in Russell until his death from cancer on August 9, 1982. Carl was married to Margaret Jackson with whom I went to school. She was much younger. Carl loved to dance and that is where they met. I was living in Winnipeg at the time going to Business College. They came to Winnipeg and decided to get married. I was Carl's best man. They had two children: Wayne and Marlene.

Wayne married Monica and they had two children. They live in Leduc, Alberta. Marlene, while working as a laboratory technician in Prince Rupert, B.C., met Dr. Herris. They were married and had two children. Ultimately, they divorced and Marlene lives in Sidney (Victoria) and works in a day care operation. My sister-in-law, Margaret, remarried and they live in Russell.

Helen went on to complete grade ten and then decided to go out working. She did housekeeping for a while and then decided to become a hairdresser. This she did for a few years and then decided to join the Air Force, to use her training. Helen was stationed in Nova Scotia until her discharge, when she came back to Winnipeg, where additional business college courses were completed and then worked for Eaton's.

While working there, she met Frederick William Hay who was attending university and then became a teacher. They were married in Winnipeg. Billy decided to work for the Canadian National Railway and became an instructor of trainmen. He served until forced to retire when a stroke affected his speech so that he could not talk. Otherwise, he was quite agile to walk and use his arms. He lived this way for seven or eight years before his demise from a heart attack.

Billy had also been a very active mason, rising to the top Grand Master. Billy had an exceptional memory and when he was well, could articulate well on any subject. He was an agnostic and we had many conversations about the Bible and the Christian Faith. When our voices would rise to a high crescendo, we would stop, for there was no way either of us was going to change. This would be repeated many times. The Masons took most of the funeral and my sister requested that I conduct a short service, including the committal.

My sister went along with Billy and became much like he was. She worked hard to keep the home and the only social life they had was the Masonic events. Both enjoyed many fishing trips with a few holiday trips to the U.S. to visit Billy's mother and aunt. Bill's dad passed away shortly after Billy and Helen were married. Helen looked after him in his last months and days. I remember what a cantankerous old man he was, feeling sorry for my sister.

Helen was not able to have children. This was the result of the illness she had when she contracted triple pneumonia while running along side the cutter in winter, as I mentioned in the previous chapter. At ten years of age, she became desperately ill. The local doctor took several pints of fluid from her and urged my mother to take her to Winnipeg for emergency treatment.

My mother took the first train, which was a three-hour ride. She grabbed a bologna sandwich and sitting toward the centre of the train coach with Helen on her lap—she headed for the Winnipeg General Hospital.

A miraculous thing took place on that journey. It happened that on their coach, there was a black lady who noticed mother who was crying and Helen who was obviously very ill. She went over to mother and said, "I see you have a very sick girl." My mother responded by telling the situation and the intended destination. The lady asked mother if she believed in prayer, and of course, as a Roman Catholic, she responded in the affirmative. The lady then asked if she could pray for my sister. With agreement by my mother, the black lady began to pray and demonstrated her enthusiasm and emotions. It was discovered later that the lady was a Pentecostal Christian and prayed with an anointing of the Holy Spirit. This, at the particular moment, startled my mother, but she appreciated the prayers and concerned support of a heaven-sent messenger.

Upon concluding her prayer, the lady said, "You are going to the General Hospital. I attend a church just behind that hospital and when your girl gets better, you come to that church. You can't miss me, as I am the only black person there. I want to know how your girl is. Meanwhile, I will ask the people of the church to pray for you and God is going to answer prayer and your little girl will be well."

An interesting thing happened right after. Helen hadn't eaten for two or three days. Right after the prayer, my sister responded and said to mother, "I'm hungry." Mother had only the bologna sandwich, but hesitated to give my sister such heavy food under the circumstances. She decided to give her a small portion, which Helen ate. They completed the journey and Helen was admitted and mother stayed with her for several days. She began to improve and my mother was able to leave the hospital and obtained some accommodation while visiting my sister. It was at this time that she was able to attend the church the lady spoke of on the train. It turned out to be "Wesley Church" that later became the now outstanding "Calvary Temple" of Winnipeg.

The miraculous thing was, during that time, mother was soundly converted to Christ, followed by water baptism and in the Holy Spirit. When she returned to Angusville, she was not able to relate some of her experiences, as the whole community was Catholic. There was a group of ladies who were called "two by two" who met in a home. Mother began to attend and received good spiritual food and fellowship. She continued to attend the Catholic Church.

It would be some years later when we had moved to Russell, that she really left the Catholic Church and became part of the small Pentecostal beginning in Russell. The occasion, when mother was in town and on her way home, she passed a vacant lot on which was pitched a large tent and she heard singing. She heard the same hymns she had heard while in Wesley Church in Winnipeg.

This was the beginning of what later became the Pentecostal Mission of Russell. The pastor of Marchwell, Saskatchewan, some 15 miles away, served as its pastor. Some of the pastors were the Parlees, Presleys, Livingstons, Rosenkes, Margaret Wilson and Hazael Chambers, Ecland and Mildred Mitchell.

Those early days included the Stiller brothers and their wives; the Swedenbergs and the Bahsler families from Marchwell, as well as the locals, Setters (relatives of evangelist Vera Ludlum), Gilmours, Zuzuks, Mrs. Charles, Charlie Rutar, Wisharts, Merritts, the MacIntoshs, the Smiths, the Mores. Folks from Binscarth and Rossburn often joined in our services. In the little mission, services were held on Sunday afternoons and I used to play for the services on the organ.

The work in Russell went through strong opposition and ridicule. Stones on its tin roof disturbed services in the McCrosty Hall. Tent meetings were disturbed and altercations took place, one resulting in a court case for assault. Services were held in the Elks Hall with the final house converted into a meeting place. Here the witness continued for many years, until the work decreased so small that it was closed in 1958. It was the year that we became pastors of Brandon and I was on the District Executive when the decision was made.

Getting back to our family history—shortly after we moved to Russell, Frank (my oldest brother) moved to Winnipeg. He was born on September 7, 1910, took some schooling, went to work with dad in Detroit and, off and on, on the farm.

Not having any interest in farming, he became a barber and had his own shop on Dagmar Street, just off Notre Dame Avenue. While he worked as a barber (haircuts in 1934 were 25 cents), Frank, who was an excellent violin player, began to play for dances. This led him to learn to play the saxophone and clarinet. He was also known as an outstanding fiddler. Frank ultimately formed his own band, called "Frank Staff and the Happy Boys." For many years he would play for events and weekend dances. This led him into a life of alcohol and loose living. I don't recall the dates, but it was during this time he married Lillian. The marriage did not last but a few years, ending in divorce. From that time, he never remarried but associated with Ann, then Flo, and finally Ethel. From his relations with Flo, a son was born, who was named Frankie. He now lives in Winnipeg.

Frank soon made his living by the orchestra and quit barbering with his last shop on Main Street, near Logan Avenue. It was here that Danny started in his barbering career. When I first came to Winnipeg, I lived with Frank and Danny in the Empire Block, at Main and Logan Avenue. Playing for dances became big business.

In partnership with others, Frank and his associates bought the Aragon Building. This housed businesses and offices in the first three floors and the top floor was the Aragon Ballroom. Here there were continual weekend dances. Frank lived in the apartment next to the ballroom and later purchased a home on Kildonan Drive in East Kildonan. He was a dedicated fisherman. With this home right on the banks of the Red River, Frank anchored his boats and the home to entertain his friends. Ultimately, he sold the Aragon Building but continued to play with his band. Toward the end of his life, he played on his own with other bands as well.

Frank was very close with his brother Mike. They were born just a year apart of each other. They often talked about their childhood and growing years and the many pranks that they played on my parents, such as cushion padding in their pants at spanking time. Also, they would dance all over the kitchen floor with the clothes washer—one of those that turned back and forth, back and forth. They were supposedly helping mother.

The last few years that Frank lived, he loved to go to Russell and go fishing with Mike. Frank had no time for anything religious and on occasion when we would talk, the subject of church would quickly deteriorate and end. It was just a few days before he passed away, I talked with him from his hospital bed and gave a few words of the need to prepare to meet God and accept Christ—telling him I was praying for him. He passed away on Tuesday, August 29, 1989 at Victoria Hospital, Winnipeg. I was not able to attend his funeral but Cheryl and Charlene were in Winnipeg at the time visiting Helen and were in attendance.

Mike was born a little over one year after Frank. He was named Mike after the firstborn who was also called Mike but died, I believe, around two years of age from pneumonia. From what I was told, Frank and Mike were close brothers, doing many things together, often getting into a lot of innocent mischief. I can't recall hearing much about Mike's growing up years. I have pictures of him in his baseball dress, as he did a lot of playing with a team they had in Angusville.

Mike did not go beyond grade 8 in school because he was needed at home to work on the farm with Dad being away so much at the Ford factory with Frank. When we moved to Russell, Mike together with Carl, were pretty well in charge of the farm. By this time, the other members began to drift in their chosen directions. I'll relate to these when I come to talk about them. Mike continued to spend a good part of the time back in Angusville working the "Brunt" farm. He lived in the small house that dad built. Mike worked very hard on this quarter section of land. Much of it was bush land and he broke up the land, pulled and burned stumps, which was not easy with the limited equipment they had in those days. It was during that time when Mike hurt his knee, which gave him a lot of discomfort throughout the rest of his life. Mike would come home to Russell on weekends to our Ledingham farm located one mile east of Russell.

At this point I would outline the arrangements that were made in respect to mother's management of the farm affairs. She felt that the two boys should take complete charge of all responsibilities. The decision was that Mike would have the Angusville farm and some of the machinery and cattle. Carl would receive the greater part of the stock and machinery and continue to rent the Ledingham farm. By this time, Frank and Helen and Danny were in Winnipeg and had no interest or claim on the family assets. I was the only other one left. I would continue to go to school and work on the farm. Carl was to provide for all my education after high school graduation. More on this later when I outline my own history.

Back to Mike.

It was during his visits to Russell that he began to court Lena Gallant who was later to become his wife, when he would ultimately sell the Angusville farm and move to farms that he would purchase and rent around Russell. One of these was the Keiper farm northwest of Russell. Here Mike lived as a bachelor until his marriage to Lena. His courtship with Lena extended over many years. My sister Helen and Lena were very close friends with unbreakable secrets. They sang in the Catholic Church choir.

Helen joined the Air Force and moved away. Mike and Lena married in November 1949. He then bought the Madill farm north of Russell and also purchased a one-half section from Frank Jones, just outside of Russell. It was on this farm that he built a house and this is where he brought Lena. It was here that they had their only child, a son, whom they named Dale. He grew up on this farm. I'll relate the record of the nieces and nephews in another section of this chapter.

Mike worked hard on those farms. He also worked with Carl on many combined projects. He made major investments in machinery and in cattle that were pastured in the Assiniboine Valley, west of Russell, next to the Saskatchewan border.

During these years, I was teaching at Bethel Bible Institute in Saskatoon. Almost every year, I went to help Mike during the harvest in August. I would drive the truck and haul grain to the elevator or to the granary and unload with a grain auger. We had great times of fun and laughs. Grace spent one of these times with me. She and Lena became close friends, which have lasted to the present time. One of the times the girls decided to have "waffles" for lunch, much to the disgust of Mike. He thought it was quite an inadequate meal for working farmers. Lena was a good support to Mike, caring for the home and during harvest, she helped by driving the grain truck.

After many years of farming, the home place was expropriated for a floodway, which placed a great part of the land under water. They decided to move into Russell. Mike had a custom home built in Brandon, which was moved into Russell and located on Memorial Boulevard, a prominent street in Russell.

Mike continued to farm from town, renting another one-half section of land. By this time Dale was through University and working. Lena would drive truck at harvest time. Mike worked a lot with Carl in combined projects and was always very kind and considerate of Carl even though it wasn't always appreciated or reciprocated.

Mike finally decided to retire. He sold all of his equipment and spent a great deal of time with friends around Russell. He was the only one of the members of our family that did some travelling. This was mostly to visit Dale in Whitehorse and us in Victoria. For a number of years they always arrived on Father's Day. On one occasion, Carl and Margaret came at the same time. We had a great time together.

Mike spent his retired years having coffee every morning with the boys at the Coffee Shop and then doing a lot of fishing, especially during the winter with his shack on the lake, doing ice fishing. We usually visited with Mike and Lena on our way to be with Helen in Winnipeg. Mike took ill with prostate cancer and for the next few years fought the disease, taking trips to Yorkton, Saskatchewan and Winnipeg, for treatments. He finally ended up in Winnipeg General Hospital for a number of weeks (or maybe months—I can't be sure). I made a trip to Winnipeg and had a beautiful visit with him. The news was not good, so Dale and Lena had to make a trip to Russell to take care of business matters.

I stayed with Mike for about three days and only left his bedside during the night where I stayed at the Science Centre by the hospital. During that time, we had many chats. I shall never forget the pain and discomfort he was enduring, even with heavy morphine treatments. We talked about many things, reminiscing about family history. I was able to share words of comfort about God, including the need to prepare to meet God. I encouraged matters of prayer and reminded him of prayers he had learned in his lifetime. Even though he never went to church or thought about spiritual things, I urged him to trust in Christ for salvation and to pray. I remember his response about praying while I was sitting on the bed. He said "I still pray."

Dale and Lena returned to Winnipeg and I returned to Vancouver, only to have Dale call me a few days later that Mike passed away. Grace and I flew to Winnipeg and motored to Russell for the funeral, which was held at Russell's St. Joseph Church on May 29, 1996. Following the internment, a reception was held in the church basement. Dale asked if I would bring a few words, which I did, paying tribute to a wonderful and perhaps favorite brother and sharing a simple bible truth. After the fellowship time, we met many old acquaintances and relatives that we hardly knew. Some of them mentioned that they had forgotten that Mike had a little brother. I will always cherish that Grace and I were able to attend.

After a brief visit with Lena and Margaret, we returned home. It was following this the realization came I was the only one left of our family. Knowing that my daughters really did not know my family history, I decided to write this auto-biography just for them. Since Mike's passing, Lena ultimately sold out at Russell and moved to Salt Spring Island, B.C., to be with Dale, Glenis and Kevin.

The next family member was Carl, who was born in Angusville in 1915. I cannot recall much of Carl's childhood upbringing. He seemed to be susceptible to almost every unique disaster situation. One time he was with dad out in the field when dad was plowing with a two-furrow plow and four horses. Carl must have been four or five years of age and was following in the furrow behind dad. He apparently was tired and laid down in the furrow and fell asleep.

Dad came around on the next round and presumed Carl had gone home. The horses and plow moved forward and the horse that always walked the furrow—old Bob—suddenly stepped out and dad looked wondering why, when suddenly he saw the sod of the plow started to cover Carl. He of course stopped and lifted Carl up and took him home. I'm sure he was grateful that "old Bob" stepped out of the furrow and missed walking on Carl. It all happened so fast, but Carl was saved from being trampled and buried beneath the sod.

I would recount another instance when Carl was saved from drowning. By the garden patch, there was an open well with about 10 feet of water in it. Mom was apparently working in the garden and Frank, Mike and Carl were playing near the well. For a second Carl was separated from Frank and Mike. He apparently stood at the edge of the well, looking into the water. All of a sudden he fell headfirst into the well. Seen by both Frank and Mike, they rushed to him. The miracle that happened was when Carl fell in. The force of the water sent him to the surface. Frank and Mike grabbed his feet and pulled him out. I presume mother was called and they were able to help Carl get his breath and expel the water. Whatever else they did, they saved Carl from a quick death. Well, Carl went on and in particular enjoyed his horse and did well in school, completing his grade eleven. Mother was always concerned that Carl get his education because, with his deformed left hand, she felt that he should do something in life that wouldn't require hard labor. The rest of the family was always told to step in and spare Carl. Well, in the end, he became a farmer and did exceptionally well.

As I mentioned earlier, mom gave to Mike and Carl the responsibility to manage the farm. With Mike on his own, mom, Carl and I carried on farming on the Ledingham farm, just east of the town of Russell. Those were the days when we purchased the first John Deere tractor on steel and when Carl purchased our first car.

As agreed, I was to help with the farm, which would provide for my future education. Mom looked after the house and I was to help her. My job was to milk the 14 cows morning and night, as Carl could not because of his hand. I shipped two 5-gallon cans of cream every week, taking it to the creamery on the bar of my bike on which I built a box affair for the can to sit on between my arms. I also helped Carl in the land work, such as haying, stooking, threshing and grain shoveling. Mother ultimately moved to town where I could complete my grade 12 and still help on the farm. The Ledingham farm was sold and Carl had to find other land. He was able to purchase a section of land about five miles west of Russell, which he farmed until retiring to Russell town.

As I previously mentioned, Carl did well on the farm, investing in machinery and raising a heard of 100 purebred Hereford cattle, which he pastured in the Assiniboine Valley. Mike used to help Carl frequently and they would consult together in all farming matters. One thing Carl enjoyed was going to the community barn dances. This was his social life in spite of his backward, shy personality and self-consciousness of his left hand.

By this time I had left for Winnipeg to attend Business College. While I was there, one weekend Carl arrived in Winnipeg with a lady friend he met at these dances. It turned out, she was a classmate of mine in high school. Her name was Margaret Jackson. They announced that they were getting married. Margaret's cousin was to be her bridesmaid and I was to be Carl's best man. They were married in a United Church on Broadway and then returned to Russell.

The folk at Russell and Inglis where Margaret's parents, brothers and relatives lived, all had a big reception for them.

Margaret was a great homemaker, a hard worker and was a tremendous help to Carl. It was from here that two children were born, Wayne and Marlene. Grace and I visited them on numerous occasions. After the children grew up and left home, Carl sold his farm, cattle and all and moved to a house he had built in Russell. He did not live too many years before he took ill. He was not well when he visited with us the one and only time in Victoria.

Wayne had trained himself in heavy duty mechanics and with his wife Monica and 2 children lived in Leduc, Alberta. Marlene had completed her training as a lab technician and was working in Prince Rupert. There she met Dr. Herris Colburne. They were married and had 2 children. It was on visiting with their R.V. at Marlene's that they came to Victoria to visit with us.

Carl, upon returning to Russell, continued with health problems with cancer of the pancreas. It was later that summer, we were in Winnipeg at Helen's when Mike, Lena, Carl and Margaret were there, Carl taking some treatments. I remember having a short visit with Carl alone and spoke to him about spiritual matters. During his high school days he came under the Gospel message. During tent meetings that were held in Russell, he was tender to the message, but later in life he lived totally with no spiritual interest. When I talked to him at Helen's, he realized his life was slipping and I can only hope and pray he made a decision for Christ. When Carl returned home, his physical condition worsened. Mike told me of the suffering Carl endured and finally on August 9, 1982, Carl passed away at 67 years of age.

Next in line was my one and only sister Helen. I cannot remember much about Helen's childhood. I have already reported on her illness. As a young girl and the miraculous restoration of healing is what brought my mother and me into Pentecost.

Helen attended school in Angusville and Russell, completing Grade 10. It was during those days when she had her close friendship with Lena. I remember as a kid, the chocolate cake she would make and top it off with icing made with pure cocoa and country cream. She worked hard on the family farm—the Matheson farm.

I recall one occasion when she was going to elope and was snatched up by her boyfriend and his helpers in a horse and cutter, because the rest of the family didn't approve of the man. I don't know how it happened, but my brothers came "to the rescue" and recaptured sister and brought her back home. She decided to join the air force and enlisted, taking up hairdressing. She was posted to Nova Scotia. I don't know exactly how long she was in the service of our country, but at the end of the war, she returned to Winnipeg, took a business course and worked for Eaton's.

It was then she met Billy Hay. He was a budding school teacher. They later married in the same United Church on Broadway Avenue where Carl and Margaret were married. They lived in the same apartment block where Frank, Danny and I lived. Bill's father lived with them.

Bill decided to take a job with the Canadian National Railway as an instructor. He worked at this job until his forced retirement and final death. They lived on Fleet Ave., in Winnipeg and then with both being in the military service, they obtained Veterans' funding and built a house on Fairmont Road in Charleswood.

Helen was a hard worker and looked after Bill in the fashion of a servant. With his shift work, she was up cooking at all hours and did everything around the house. When we were pastoring in Brandon we had frequent visits with them, as well as my mother. Mom had now moved to Winnipeg from Russell and had been there many years. When she moved to Winnipeg she was a faithful attendee of Calvary Temple. I shall write concerning mother's closing days at the end of this family chapter.

I have already mentioned much about Helen. She considered me her favorite brother. She seemed to have a special gift to fight with the other brothers. I suppose that didn't help because they would never restrain themselves from antagonizing her. I tried to overlook matters and never argue with her, but endeavored to show love and understanding. As a result, Helen would often put to practice some of the advice I suggested in a spirit of kindness. Because of this amicable relationship, she depended on me. In our frequent visits she demonstrated warm hospitality and generosity. When she was ill or had a problem, she would phone asking if I could come immediately. This was not possible but she felt she could count on me.

Helen's life from the time she was ill, which resulted in mother's conversion, is of interest. Bill worked hard on the railroad and Helen looked after him like a baby, doing everything conceivable to keep him happy and well fed. He was not always as kind and loving as a husband should be, but they managed to sustain a solid marriage. Both were very kind to us and whenever we were in Winnipeg, we always stayed with Helen and Bill. They particularly loved our girls, Cheryl and Charlene. The girls were able to visit with Aunt Helen and they were there with her the very day she passed away.

As I have already indicated, Bill had a stroke, which caused him to lose his speech and he endured this for at least seven years before his death with a heart attack. We would visit them annually. And, at the time of his death, were able to help with all arrangements. Helen requested that I would speak at the service and conduct the internment. Bill's brother Bud, his daughter and her husband, came from Victoria. After the funeral, the folk took the boat and trailer and some other of Bill's things and returned to Victoria.

Helen continued to live in the house. She enjoyed times with some of her neighbors such as John, Mary and Patsy. She began to have health problems of one kind or another. Frank would often come to her place with Chinese food and they would enjoy themselves. Whenever we came to visit, Frank would pick me up at the airport and we would visit with her and with Marion and family.

As time passed, Helen evidenced serious health problems. Grace and I journeyed home. We stopped at Mike and Lena's for a couple of days and then via phone call from Helen, hastened to Winnipeg, as she was gravely ill. Upon our arrival we found that she could not eat. She had become very nauseated and had lost weight. We took her to the doctor for tests, x-rays and examination at the medical arts building in downtown Winnipeg. In the doctor's office, Grace had to dress her, as she was so weak and thin. On the way home, she insisted on doing some banking business, which in the end proved necessary. In a few days, she was admitted to Grace Hospital. We visited with her daily, staying in her apartment at the Wellesley.

I might inject here that a couple of years before this time, when visiting Helen, she felt that she could not manage to keep up the house on Fairmont. With great reluctance, she listed it and one Sunday while we were at church, she received and signed a sale of the house. Then began the dismantling of the home, selling many items, selling the car and arranging all the errands of business, banking, and legal matters.

Helen had checked out the Wellesley in Charleswood and the one on Portage Avenue, which she ultimately took. It was here that she enjoyed lovely living for some years during which we continued our visits with her.

As I have already related, it was from here she was admitted to Grace Hospital where she passed away. We had been there before returning to Vancouver, so Cheryl and Charlene went to visit Aunt Helen. They stayed in her apartment and visited with her right to the very day she died.

On that day they were with her, doing her hair and attending to her. They left to get a bite to eat and while away, were contacted that Helen had passed away. It seemed that she was satisfied to see the girls and was now ready to die. The girls were not able to stay for the funeral and left for home after we arrived. Helen was a great sister and I was able to dismantle her apartment and as executor of her will, was able to conclude her affairs. Some items our family took and the rest we sold or gave to Sharon and Marion.

The next member of the family is Danny who was five years older than me. I can't recall much of Danny's early life. He terminated going to school at Grade 10. He went to work in a lumber camp so he wasn't home too much. I understand that at work, he wore a heavy winter cap and with heavy perspiration sort of scalded his scalp, which resulted in an early loss of his hair. In his teens, at home his friend was Lawson McIntosh. Both did go to church and Danny made a decision for Christ. He was baptized in water in a creek, which ran through our Matheson Farm in Russell.

I was there at the time and recall the Roman Catholic priest greatly upset about some of our family leaving the church. We were gathered at the bridge that crossed the creek, which was fairly deep and there were many people gathered and the priest was there as well. When Danny was in the water with Rev. Parlee, the priest shouted "Danny come out of there". Everyone thought that he was calling a dog in the water to come out and paid no attention to the baptism.

Finally Danny was baptized and when he was, the priest stormed away, got into his car and drove away rather madly, almost hitting some people. Danny, with Lawson, did attend one year at a bible school, which Rev. Parlee held in the church at Marchwell, Saskatchewan, just 14 miles away from Russell. But Danny's life drifted away from the Lord. He moved to Winnipeg to be with Frank and become a barber. He worked with Frank and then had his own shop on Osborne Street. By this time, I was living with Frank and Danny in the Empire Building on Logan Avenue.

Danny became an excellent violinist and like Frank, began to play for dances, finally getting his own orchestra. He took to drinking and became a heavy smoker. During this time, he was courting Marion Bodnar, whom he married and then built a house in East Kildonan. He gave up barbering and went to work for Imperial Oil plant not far from where they lived. He drove a big tanker truck. Their family consisted of Judy, Robbie, Sharon and Roddie.

I recall visiting them with Mum, Helen and Bill and our girls. I took some 8 mm film on that occasion. When the kids were in their teens, Danny took sick. He also had to have an operation on his knee. I don't know the sequence of time, but I understand because of being a heavy smoker, he developed a cancerous condition in his lungs. It was when he had the knee operation that he hemorrhaged and suddenly died.

We were in Kitchener at that time and I flew back for the funeral. I remember I wanted to see Danny at the funeral home. Frank and Mike said I should not because of how Danny looked, but I insisted. Danny, encased in a plastic bag, was in the casket. In the hemorrhaging, his blood exploded throughout the body and he was almost totally black. They could not do any embalming. It was sad to see him, but I was glad to be able to see him even in such a condition. Danny passed away at 51 years of age, the same age as dad, when he died of throat cancer.

I will insert here Dad's passing. Dad developed ill health as a heavy smoker. When he was building the house at Angusville, he contracted a cold and a cancer growth on his throat. He had some treatments in Winnipeg but ultimately a growth, the size of a large apple, developed on the front of his neck. Dad could not look after himself so he came to Russell.

The cancer growth had to be dressed every day and mother would nurse him. The growth was very open and vicious looking. Mother used to put a piece of raw meat against it, which the cancer would eat up. It was quite the process, but it kept dad alive for a time. He lost his voice completely and was in a lot of pain. I presume he must have been taking some pain medication.

I remember the last Saturday of June 1936. Frank, Dan, Helen and Carl had all gone to town for the great Saturday night when all the farmers gathered and the whole community came together. Upstairs, dad was in great distress and rapped on the night table for mum to come. Mike was there at the time and mum asked if he would stay with her. I was 11 years old at the time.

We were up in the room when dad could hardly breathe. I remember he asked mum to hold him up in a sitting position in bed. I saw my father's body suddenly jerk. He passed away in mum's arms at the age of 51 years. Mike went into town to get the rest of the family. Then came the preparations for the funeral.

We could not afford the funeral home looking after things so my brothers and relatives came and took charge. Dad was dressed and placed on a wooden flat in the living room while the men proceeded to build a casket and cover it with material. The day of the funeral a flat deck truck carried the casket to the church and ultimately to the burial. I don't recall much of the service in the Catholic Church nor the events and gathering of friends and relatives. Dad was buried in the Russell Cemetery. Regretfully, I never knew what it was like to have a Dad.

Just a conclusion regarding Danny. His family continued to live in East Kildonan. Judy lived for a time in Vancouver and then back in Winnipeg. Robbie married and worked with his mother who by now had a very successful restaurant business with a deli in North Winnipeg. Sharon married, divorced and remarried and worked with Marion in the deli (she was especially good to Aunt Helen) and Roddie married and lives in East Kildonan. With the exception of Judy, they all have children but I don't know exactly how many or their names.

The last addition to this family is "yours truly." I relate some of my early years growing up as a farm boy and what ultimately led to Christian ministry.

I always appreciate growing up to learn the value of work and responsibility. Being on the farm I did not have opportunity to be involved in sports and community events. My tasks were to milk 14 cows by hand, separate milk, ship cream and work farm duties like haying, threshing, driving horses and farming land. It was school in the morning and home right after to do chores. Summer holidays were exceptionally busy times. My memories abound with the exciting and educational learning and events, which only a farm boy could experience.

My particular friends were Bill and Bob McIntosh, Walter Wishart, Clayton Merritt and others. We had many happy social times. It was in the McIntosh home where I learned about the Christian walk. I was a Catholic boy and served as an altar boy as part of our family religion. Because of my mother's conversion, the teaching of Laura McIntosh (my only Sunday School teacher), I accepted Christ as Savior, received the baptism of the Holy Spirit and was baptized in the Assiniboine river. This part of my young life probably led to entering Christian service. I had a great childhood.

# Chapter 3

## *Launching and Learning*

I was the last of the family. Born on July 31, 1925 on the Brunt farmhouse outside of Angusville. It was the same house that I mentioned before, which burned down at that potato-digging bee.

My childhood was spent moving around with the family. I played with the various neighbour kids, especially the Kodloski's. I started school in Angusville. My first teacher was Miss Clarke. I was 6 years old. I don't know exactly why, but I was put into grade two half way through the first year. My teacher was Miss Gertrude Staples, daughter of the local station agent. When I was in grade 4, we moved to Russell and it was here I completed high school, graduating in June 1941 at 16 years of age (of course I turned 17 the next month),

In the fall I moved to Winnipeg where I went to Dominion Business College and completed my junior accountancy. I lived with Frank and Danny. I used to have lunch at the Jolly Canuck in the Bay where cousin Vera Woreneski and relative Ann Derkatch worked. I used to sell tickets for Frank at his dance events.

When I turned 18, I received a call to the army as the war was still on. I decided that I was not for army life so I joined the Navy. I became a Writer in Sickbay looking after records and secretarial work. Of course I had to take all the medical training as well, taking my turn with the medical personnel. These included Drs' Whitley, McCallum and McCoy, Chief Charlie Menzies and sick berth attendants Joe Sowtis, Bill Ringer, Harry Hanna, Harry Young and myself.

There were many interesting experiences during those two or more years when we were stationed at "Chippawa", Winnipeg. Some were pretty gross but others were interesting, learning medical know how, e.g. diagnosing appendix attacks or perforated ulcer or giving penicillin shots to VD boy's. I did not live on barracks but continued with Frank and Danny in the Empire Block on Logan Avenue.

Being in the navy, I wanted to see the world and tried to get drafted to the coast and maybe out to sea. Chief Menzies, who liked my work and wanted to keep me, thwarted any effort I made. Finally the European War ended and recruitment was being made for the Pacific war with Japan. Thinking this was my chance, I (the only one from Sick Bay) signed up for the Pacific. They gave everyone 30 days leave, plus I had accrued 14 days annual leave, so I went on 44 days of unencumbered military liberty after which I was to be posted to Australia.

However, half way through my leave, the war in Japan ended with VJ day and that ended any transfer. I returned to barracks to work with the discharges that started. Being part of the team, we would be the last to be discharged as all the round riggers (bellbottom uniforms) had to be done first. The rest of us (square riggers) would be done last.

During my time in Winnipeg, I attended Calvary Temple, participating in many activities, lighthouse mission services and social gatherings. When the wars folded, there were a number of service personnel in the church all working on discharge efforts. A number were planning to go to Bible College and some to university.

Some of my closer friends like Ed Lother, Benson Berry, Ernie Peterson, Paul Malm and others, decided on Western Bible College and I decided to join them. It would mean that we could get out of the services and not have to wait until everyone else was out first. So I applied for discharge, having been accepted at WBC.

I would use my gratuities for college fees and books and be allowed living allowance for the next three years. Back at navy barracks because of my position, I would not be able to get out in time for school. I had a stroke of good fortune when I began my discharge routine. I had to tour the various departments to have my 'chit' signed beginning with sickbay. The medical officer was Dr. Whitley.

When I went in to see him, he said we couldn't get out till the rest, so I really can't sign your slip. My tour would have ended right there but Dr. Whitley said "don't let on you know, but I am getting out myself to tend to my practice in Victoria, B.C., and my ailing mother, so it doesn't matter to me if you leave." So, he signed my chit and I was away, much to the disgust of my compatriots, saying I had pulled some sort of coup and questioned how come I got away with it.

In any case, I was given 30 days discharge leave and could start college while still in the navy. Thirty days later, I went for my final discharge routine and had a lot of fun joking with my fellow SBA's. Anyway, it was nice to get 74 days of leave pay, which was really not that great but it was something.

Three years of Bible College were interesting times.

We were housed in the basement of Calvary Temple. In our first year there, 65 of us packed into the old band room. Our teachers were Dr & Mrs. Purdie, Dr & Mrs. Sweet, Professor Baker, Miss Lemon, Miss Siemans, Alvin Shindel, Les Holdcroft, Bernard Embree, Riley Kaufman and Watson Argue.

For our second year, the Edmonton College was opened up by Rev. Buntain and reduced our class with the Alberta students going there. As it turned out, we graduated with the largest class that the college ever had with 35 graduates.

During the first year, the composition of the class included the meek and mild souls as well as those of us who had been in the services or the working world. Miss Lemon, Dean of Women, had quite a time coping with these people who were not too cooperative with the rules and regulations. Dr Purdie would respond by saying "you never can tell". The teachers were unique in many ways. Dr. Purdie, a former Anglican, was a sound teacher, grounding us in objective truths.

Dr. Sweet was very quaint, with his wig and side burns that were glued on and when the temperature was high, the glue would melt and trickle down the side of his face. He was the teacher that gave 99% and 100% for every exam. His wife was a sister of the famous Nellie McLune, a writer and poet. Mrs. Sweet was teaching English and would always be quoting poetry and prose.

Professor Baker with his goatee, a professor from St. John's College, taught "Life of Christ" and his blackboard notes were not understandable, if you happened to miss class. Alvin Schindel taught Prophets and General Epistles. Les Holdcroft taught Pentateuch, History and Geography. Watson Argue taught Homiletics and public speaking. Riley Kauffman was the music instructor.

We all lived on our own, as the school had no dormitory. At noon we frequented the corner store for corn beef sandwiches. Many of us fellows went every Wednesday to the YMCA and during the winter we played hockey every Monday afternoon. Those of us who were part of the Calvary Temple activities did not sit with the student body at church services.

During our second and third years, we held classes in a block next door that the college purchased. Between school years I did vacation Bible School in Southern Manitoba (Mylor, Mather, etc) and went home to Russell to help on the farm.

Our graduation was held in May 1948 at the church. Our graduation banquet was held in the Royal Alexander Hotel (CPR). That was the occasion when Professor Baker, who was a bachelor, recounted his three-time engagement to 3 girls, boasting that the "Lord delivered me from them all".

In anticipation of the future (Grace and I were going together and planning marriage), contact was made with Rob Argue about going to teach at Bethel Bible Institute in Saskatoon. Inasmuch as Ruth (Rob's wife) was her sister, I guess this was of influence in the favorable decision to give me a teaching position, which was to be combined with a small pastorate, all approved by the District. This was the month of May and school would not be opened till September, so I planned to launch my ministry, leaving Winnipeg for my new pastoral charge.

# Chapter 4

## *Beginning the Journey*

I remember making plans to leave for Asquith, Saskatchewan, a town about 25 miles west of Saskatoon. I then went and purchased a trunk to pack up all my belongings as I was going by train (we still have that trunk).

I had made contact with one of the members of the church who was to meet me when I arrived. It was late afternoon when I pulled in to Asquith and was met by Mr. Reilly, a jolly Irishman. We were able to get my trunk to the living quarters over the church. Then we were hosted for supper at Bro. & Sis. Reilly's home. She was a very kind hostess and a good cook. After a time of hearing many interesting and humorous stories told by Mr. Reilly, I went back to the church and settled into the living quarters.

Entrance to the quarters was made from the back veranda up a flight of stairs. I was quite impressed with the expanse of this fully furnished apartment. There was a fully equipped kitchen (minus a fridge), dining room, a living room and two bedrooms. It was actually very nice and clean. Just off the kitchen, there was a dumb waiter, which descended to the bottom of the veranda. This was used to keep things cool.

The next day I went to shop for food and began to analyze my situation. I mentioned my dumb waiter cooler. I had opened a can of "Klick" for lunch and put the balance in a dish with a saucer covering it. Pulling it up at supper to finish the "Klick" I lifted the saucer and my meat was covered with maggots. I soon learned what was not to be put in the dumb waiter, but I did learn to batch and visit the congregation for a good meal including Mrs. Kosick.

The church was on the main floor, seating about 25 to 40 people. A small platform at the front and a pump organ. My main contact was with the Ruthven family. There were Mr. &

Mrs. Ruthven, daughter Mae and son Will. The Ruthven's were the main supporters of the work. They had a small dairy herd and shipped milk.

The congregation was made up of the Ruthvens, Reilleys, Ridsdales, Mrs Kosick—a total of 9 people. The oldest people were in their 70's and the youngest was Will Ruthven (45 years old). There were no children to have a Sunday School. The Baptist church had all the kids from the town and community. There was an occasional visitor to our service, held on Sunday at 11:00 am. There was no evening or midweek service. We had a street meeting every Saturday night. It was the big community gathering. We used a little portable pump organ and conducted a service singing hymns. After stretching our vocal chords, we then preached a salvation message.

We had a sizeable listening audience, being located beside the main store of the town. I am sure we would have 75 to 100 people, as some would come and go, and others stopped by. These meetings were not too encouraging because we really saw no results. At least we planted the seed and maybe eternity will reveal some results. The audiences were very polite and attentive as there were never any disturbances.

I remember May Ruthven commenting one time how a previous pastor (Reuben Swanson) said after his meeting while packing up and having no response, "makes you feel like saying, 'well folk if you want to go to hell, go ahead.'" Knowing Reuben, he was just that type of blunt person, having associated with him in Abbotsford where he retired. He was part of my congregation when I served as interim pastor for 9 months.

The little congregation was very faithful and supportive. The Ruthven family was very kind. They gave me one of their cars to use from time to time for visitation and travel into Saskatoon to Bethel Bible Institute, where I would be on the teaching staff in the coming fall.

I well recall my first service. Not knowing anyone but the Reilly's, I did not know who to call on for anything. So I proceeded to welcome all. There were 2 or 3 other people in attendance. I announced the first hymn, then went to the pump organ and played for the singing. It was time for prayer, so I prayed. I made what little announcements there were, then received the offering.

Not knowing who the usher was or who were the leaders, I proceeded to take the tin pie plate on the little table in front of the pulpit and took up the offering—sometimes with 3 quarters on the plate. We sang some more hymns, after which I spoke and closed in prayer. In 54 years of ministry, this was the only service where I did everything. I soon found out that Bro. Ruthven and Bro. Ridsdale were the board members and May Ruthven was the treasurer. From then on, Will Ruthven was my head (only) usher. We had some good meetings and rich fellowship with these great people. I will always cherish the memory of them as I know that all have gone to be with the Lord.

It was during these early months that I was associated with Elim Tabernacle and Pastor & Mrs. Robert Donnelly. We got to know some of the wonderful people of the congregation: folk like the McLeods, Klassens, Fords, Graffins, Burts, Chernicks, Fasts, Mrs. Hornby senior, C.B. Doerrs (the great soloist) just to name a few.

In those days the congregation was not large, having gone through a serious split during the latter rain movement. We sought to help the Donnelly's and were helped in turn by the younger people like Phyllis Graffin, Lois Burt, Rosemary Chernick, Ada Campbell, Art Fast in our street meetings and some services.

When in Saskatoon I stayed with the Donnelly's and their children, Ralph and Ruthella. Bro. Donnelly was a fabulous preacher, a real prince of a man and we helped with his broadcast "the Wonderful Word".

During this time, I was introduced to the District Superintendent, Rev. Eric Hornby and his family, Allon, Ruth and Rose, with whom I would have a future association. I also met the principal of Bethel, Rev. R.M. Argue, when later we became brothers-in-law. I also met Rev. & Mrs. Gordon McQuarrie and Rev. & Mrs. Peter Walker—all of whom were on the faculty of Bethel. It would be my joy and privilege to be part of the staff, which lasted for six years. I also served on the District Youth Executive for a number of years, being part of promoting youth activities in the district and raising missionary funds for overseas projects.

While pastoring Asquith, I began to work at Bethel preparing for my lecture responsibility as well as preparing the school facilities. Ultimately, I served my pastorate from my one room in Bethel for about 2 years, using students to take some of the services. One couple that used to come and help were Ed and Genevieve Chamberlain, who later were part of my congregation at Semans, Saskatchewan. The Asquith church was taken over by Pastor & Mrs. Alex Harper and by Irvine and Bernice Fuhrman.

Around 1951 I assisted Bro. Donnelly with the choir music on the broadcast as well as in the church. In the Donnelly story—Songs of the Reapers—(published by the PAOC Saskatchewan District) Brother Donnelly wrote: "I think it was during the year of 1951 that Brother E. Austin was my assistant and he was a great blessing to the assembly." It was also during that year that a number of outstanding miracles of healing occurred. Some folk who listened to the "Wonderful Word" broadcast would bring in a sick person and almost without exception, a healing would take place. I have a clear recollection of working with Brother Austin, painting the inside of Elim Tabernacle. Some folk came in looking for the pastor, so we came down from the scaffold and went with them to their car, where we prayed for a young woman who was quite ill. They went on their way to the doctor, but by the time they got there the young lady was well."

We enjoyed serving with the Donnelly's and saw many results from his outstanding preaching ministry. I would also pay tribute to him as an exceptional man of God. His was a unique ministry empowered by the Holy Spirit and from his ability to prepare his messages from a total library of his Bible, a concordance and a dictionary. I recall one message when he preached about sin and to emphasize sin, he used a tirade of eight or ten adjectives to describe sin. He was a prince of preachers.

I had the honor of eulogizing him at his funeral service in Penticton many years from the time we worked with him and had him share evangelistic services in a number of places where we pastored. We could speak of many other beautiful associations with Elim and the Donnelly's. While there I was also a member of the Wonderful Word broadcast quartet with Les Halliwall, John and Keith Wright and myself. Grace was on the Christ's Ambassadors executive youth of Elim.

# The Great Wedding

During our 6 years of association with Elim and Bethel Bible Institute I want to relate the greatest event that ever took place in my life apart from my conversion. Grace and I were married in Winnipeg on Sept. 3, 1949. She had moved to Saskatoon with her mother in the fall of 1948.

Our wedding was a beautiful event. We traveled from Saskatoon so we could be married in our home church in Winnipeg—Calvary Temple. Upon arrival, we stayed with our good friends, Dr, and Mrs. Lorne Carson. Dr. Carson was our dentist when we lived in the city and were part of a long lasting friendship and church association.

Plans were to be married on Saturday with a reception to follow at Peggy's Pantry on Portage Avenue. We had previously arranged to have our banns published in the church. Grace's brother-in-law, Rev. Robert Argue was doing the ceremony.

When he got to checking into things, he discovered that the pastor had not made any banns announcement or filed the necessary forms. Rob phoned us in panic and it necessitated that we rush from East Kildonan to city hall in Winnipeg to get a license. Fortunately we made it before noon closing and got our license ($10 for license and $10 for late application).

Back to E. Kildonan to get ready for the wedding. Jean Carson was a tremendous help and inspiration in the midst of the panic. The wedding went off without a hitch (oh yes we were hitched).

The bridal party included Grace's Maid of Honor, Dorothy Carson, with my sister Helen as attendant and Judy Argue as flower girl. My best man was Vance Carson and my usher was Norman Swanson. Bessie Oke was organist and

Inga Thorenson was soloist. Grace was brought down the aisle by her brother David. I can't recall how many guests there were but it was a nice sized group.

I don't remember too much about the reception at Peggy's Pantry. It was a nice gathering and dinner. Traditionally when the couple left receptions, they were shadowed by fun filled friends and sometimes invaded the honeymoon. Vance did us a favor by getting our car parked at the back lane. When Grace threw her bouquet, we exited out the back door. Vance drove us to the Royal Alexander Hotel, then parked the car, came back with the keys and said, "have fun!"

Vance was a close friend and we had numerous times together in previous years. We spent our honeymoon at Carson's trailer in the Lake of the Woods areas near Kenora, Ont. Then we returned to Saskatoon in our 1946 Studebaker, which needed regular stops to keep filling up a leaking radiator. Arriving safely, we resumed our life in Saskatoon.

Now—a little more about Bethel Bible School days.

Grace worked for the Federal government in the Veterans land act department until we were married. She continued until May of 1950. During the summer when there was no school, we traveled for a period of time in evangelism with Les Halliwell, holding services at Glaslyn & Sonningdale. We also went to Russell to help my brother harvest. Another summer we traveled with the school quartet (Robert, Ed, Grace and Les Halliwell, Ruth Bitz and Frilly Beaumont) promoting the school and raising funds in 1951.

During that tour we traveled in one car over 10,000 miles going into Alberta, Saskatchewan, Manitoba, N/West Ontario and into Minnesota. It would take too long to relate our experiences with a service each night in a different place. One church was full of the Wolf's—another with a bee disturbing the service—another arrived through muddy roads with our car literally covered with mud, which we drove right into the lake to wash.

What a time we had. We invariably landed in a place, changed in one place or the church baptistery and were billeted at another place for the night and then it was off for the next service miles away. It was quite an experience to sleep in the strangest places and eat a variety of foods. Our hosts in every place were most friendly and kind, considering our close fellowship in the car and long miles.

We completed the tour with the best of happy associations and happy memories. Every church and pastor welcomed us warmly and received the ministry music of the quartet with my wife at the piano. Principal Rob excelled with dynamic ministry of the Word. We promoted Bethel Bible Institute well.

Right on campus, I must relate some interesting things that happened. I should mention that the school was constructed through a steadfast faith that God would lay it on the hearts of others to rally around it with their financial support. The buildings, however, were not the greatest but served the purpose. The main building was three stories, with the men on the top floor, ladies on the second with the Deans living at either end, and the basement for married couples, laundry facilities, library and canteen (the Nook). The classrooms and dining hall were housed in an L-shaped building.

At the back of the main building there was a residence where the Argues and Austins lived. Our quarters were on the second floor, using the bedrooms, with the kitchen being the two closets between the rooms.

Our water supply and sewer pipes came from the rear of the main building through a circulation route under the ground. Also, the heating came in the same way and when the furnace was fired up, we knew heat was coming with the sound of cannon fire.

One winter, our pipes froze and we had to dig a manhole, using a hose with hot water from the heating system to unthaw our pipes. That was one Sunday that Rob and I spent the day with the sewer system.

The dining hall seated the students and faculty at tables of 6. During our time there, Jean Olson was our cook and the students were assigned various duties on campus. The meals were plain and supplies came from donations of food, meat, vegetables from many farmers. One thing the dining hall and kitchen were plagued with was rats. Actually the whole city one year was plagued with rats, but that's another story.

As a staff member, we were continually doing work as carpenters, plumbers, electricians and painters. Yes, we taught theology also. All the school personnel, in spite of many adverse conditions, sustained a beautiful spirit of love, unity, co-operation and participation. Classes and chapel services saw great moves of the Holy Spirit and all were there ready to learn and be equipped to do exploits for God.

The faculty were not there because of the money. I remember my first pay was $5.00 per week plus food. The dedication of Bro. Argue and other teachers was outstanding. In retrospect, some of our greatest leaders of the Pentecostal Assemblies of Canada were graduates of Bethel.

## Bethel Bible Institute

It was in 1948 that I graduated from Western Bible College and moved to Asquith. As already indicated, I joined the faculty of Bethel Bible Institute in the fall of 1948. The faculty included Rev & Mrs. Robert (Ruth) Argue, Rev & Mrs. Peter Walker, Rev & Mrs. Gordon McQuarrie, Rev. R. Donnelly, Mr. Ed Lother (we were in the navy at the same time). We had a graduating class of six and 25 undergraduates. In later years, while we were still on Bethel's faculty, the student body rose to 48 then 69 and so on. We served with other faculty members such as Alvin Schindel, Rev. G.H. Stiller, Herb Barber, May English, Cora Grafham, E.L. Moore, Grace Brown, Don Waggoner, Rev & Mrs. Ken Davis and Emily Gurr.

During my years I taught Christian Education subjects, Homiletics, Bible history and Geography, English, music theory and conducting, Pentateuch, Thessalonians, as well as supervising buildings and grounds and overseeing practical assignments.

It was during the last two years while still teaching at Bethel, that we became the pastor of the Semans congregation. We traveled every second week and spent 2 days of intensive lectures and conducting choral music with the student body. This involved leaving on a Monday at 4:00 am by train and returning on Tuesday evening. It was a pretty heavy load but we did appreciate being able to continue college working as well as pastoral ministry.

I will conclude this chapter with our ministry in Semans Saskatchewan. This town was located about the middle between Saskatoon and Regina. The community with a population of about 850 people surrounded by many large family farms. The town had several general stores, a large hardware and lumber store, numerous garages, restaurants and service stores.

The Pentecostal assembly had been founded for many years and the little church was called "the Semans Chapel". A long list of pastors over the years served the assembly. When we took over, we followed Rev and Mrs John Larson. The assembly had sustained an honourable witness in the community and when we arrived the small congregation anticipated additional growth.

We moved from Saskatoon shortly after school closing in 1952. The residence next to the church was a little four-room cottage. One of the first things to be done was to have kitchen cupboards installed. A man was hired and for the next weeks we endured construction noise and sawdust.

At that time, my wife was expecting Cheryl to be born in December. The sawdust made my wife very ill so we did have our problems. The bedroom had a bed, a dresser and closet. The living room furnished with old furniture and an oil-burning heater. The kitchen had an old fashioned stove, kitchen table and chairs. The little back room was the bathroom with a 'biffy'. There was a nice back yard with a small car garage at the rear by the lane.

The town site had only one well for our water supply. Mr. Water Wagon came by twice a week and we were able to purchase water at six cents a pail, which we stored in a large crock in the kitchen. Mr. Water Wagon was also the 'honeybucket' man who once a week came around to collect our 'biffy' sewage. He did use a different wagon.

We decided quickly that it was necessary to build an outside 'biffy' by the garage especially for the summer months, because the congregation children used our facility. However, winter was another thing so it was back in the washroom.

With no water and no sewage, we decided to dig a well in the small cellar under the house. We shaped it like a large bottle, and a man from the community plastered the interior so that after many coats and fine troweling, it was like a glass bottle.

Then we installed a hand pump and caught rain from the house and church roof, which could fill the bottle well. We had to make sure to disconnect the spouts when the well was full. This actually was finalized just before we left Semans, so I think I used the pump once.

As I mentioned, Grace was expecting in December when Cheryl was born on Dec. 25, 1952. We traveled that early morning to Nokomis, 18 miles away where the hospital was located. It was a long day because Cheryl didn't arrive until late evening. The hospital was a large home and that day there were no patients. The staff was very kind by serving Grace and me a turkey and ham meal for supper. Dr Weiss had to be called from Semans around 8:00 pm and delivered our little girl. I remember when he came out of the delivery room, all perspired and said let's have a drink, which we did with ginger ale from the kitchen fridge.

We had a look at our baby with her pile of hair and a ribbon and happy that things went well. That Christmas day we were invited to Irvine and Hilda Chamberlain's home for dinner and had to inform them from Nokomis we could not make it. I returned home that night and went to their farm with the news. They were a great family with 8 children, a hired man and a maid. An interesting item was that the youngest—little Elaine about 5 or 6—insisted that my chair at the table be saved for my arrival.

After a week, I brought Grace and Cheryl home and the related tasks were quickly assumed. As I previously mentioned, water was scarce, so we bought a few large blocks of ice, which were melted in a boiler on the stove. This water was to wash the diapers, etc. Grace did a valiant job under the circumstances, seeing she never knew anything but the convenience provided in a city dwelling.

The congregation was small and the little chapel could seat about 75 or 80 people. We applied ourselves to pastoring, visiting and in the short 2 years there saw the congregation increase to 65 to 70 people. We conducted Sunday school, worship and gospel evening services as well as a mid-week Bible study and prayer service.

We saw God bless with entire families coming into the church. We finally constructed an addition to the church building for Sunday School and other activities such as vacation bible school. We were also blessed with a nice group of young people.

A number of United Church people came to the church and the Pastor said to me, "You're emptying my church." One of the families included the town policeman. We had many social gatherings and lots of fun and fellowship. Some of the names were the Chamberlin's, Dennis', McConnels', Greenshields, Beelers, Beugs, Griffiths, Curral, McLelands, Hillis, Hodges and others I can't remember.

The congregation gave us what support they could. In order to supplement our resources, I took a job doing books at the North American Lumber Company and Hardware Store. However, the folk regularly filled our drawer in the locker plant with lots of meats. Another event that took place here was our filling in for the Williams' in Brandon, Manitoba which probably was why we later were called from North Vancouver to be their Pastor. We enjoyed our brief time in Semans. After two years (1952-1954) we were invited to pastor Vernon B.C.

Left: Ed's parents.

Right: Ed with his brothers Frank and Mike.

Left: The house in which Ed was born.

Above: Ed's boyhood pal Rex. Below: Ed in the navy in World War II.

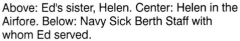

Above: Ed's sister, Helen. Center: Helen in the Airfore. Below: Navy Sick Berth Staff with whom Ed served.

Above: Ed and Grace in their courting days.

Left: Ed's Bible College grad picture

Below: The weddding of Charlene and Mark.

Above: Grace and Ed's Wedding Day, September 2, 1949.

Right: Ed's brother Carl & his 2 children.

Below: The Austin daughters, Cheryl and Charlene.

Left: Ed and his brother, Danny. Above: Ed's first pastorate at Asquith.

Above: Bethel Bible Institute where Ed taught for 6 years.

Left: Pastor and Mrs. Austin after years of fruitful ministry.

The church which Ed and Grace pastored in Semans.

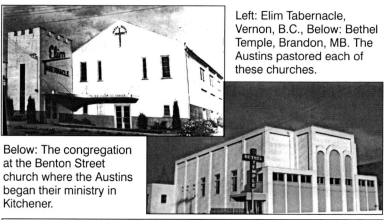

Left: Elim Tabernacle, Vernon, B.C., Below: Bethel Temple, Brandon, MB. The Austins pastored each of these churches.

Below: The congregation at the Benton Street church where the Austins began their ministry in Kitchener.

Below left: A model of the church that was built in Kitchener under the Austin's ministry. Right: Ed with his "Fifty Years of Ministry" certificate.

Above: A portion of the congregation that gathered for the dedication of the new Kitchener Gospel Temple in 1968.

Left: A sketch of Calvary Temple, Kamloops, where the Austins pastored after Kitchener.

Right: Dedication of Victoria's new Glad Tidings church.

Below: Connaught Heights in New Westminster.

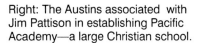

Right: The Austins associated with Jim Pattison in establishing Pacific Academy—a large Christian school.

Left: Pastor Ed Austin*

Below: Grace Austin**

Left:
Ed with
grand-
son
Aaron.

*Pictured when he was on the pastoral staff of Broadway Church of Vancouver.

**Ed enthusiastically describes her as "the greatest Pastor's wife!"
Left: A later picture of Aaron Edward.

# Chapter 5

## *Ministry Stations*

As part of our call to the work of the ministry, was the innate understanding that the field is the world, predicated on the commission of our Lord to go into ALL THE WORLD to preach the gospel. Just as the church house is not to be confined as the place where the gospel is preached, so too is the recognition that believers in local assemblies need a variety of ministry to lead them into the pastures of Christian maturity.

In each place we have been given the privilege to serve God's people of like precious faith, we have followed in the spirit of 1 Corinthians 3:6-8: "So neither he who plants nor he who waters is anything, but only God, who makes things grow. The man who plants and the man who waters have one purpose, and each will be rewarded according to his own labor."

Those who either preceded us in a ministry station, or those who followed us, are stewardship-partners of the manifold grace of God. Each place of ministry has been both rewarding and challenging.

### Vernon, B.C.

The call to Vernon B.C. was very unusual and unique. It was while pastoring in Semans we had the honour of a visit from the General Superintendent of the PAOC. He was Walter McAlister and with his visit my respect and appreciation of him went very high. He didn't think it too humbling to visit my small assembly. I believe that it was probably through his recommendation that we were contacted to consider coming to Vernon.

The retiring pastor was Einar Domeij who asked if we would consider being voted on to come. I say our eventual going there was unique because we had never been there nor asked to preach for a call. Sight unseen and from recommendations we were called by the congregation.

We concluded our time in Semans in June 1954. We packed all our belongings in our car—personal and breakables and shipped some by freight. We enjoyed our brief time in Semans and the congregation was sorry to see us depart.

The journey to British Columbia was most interesting and rather unnerving at times. We had never been west of Calgary and never had driven in the mountains. We took the Southern US route and traveled through Glacier National Park heading toward the Oroville, Ossoyos entrance into B.C. Traveling through Glacier, we started our entrance by pulling into a gas station and filling up with cheap regular gas. We were not far into climbing mountain highways when we discovered we did not have enough power to make the climb. We traveled for some time doing the best to use up the cheaper gas until we could get a good quality of new fuel. Pulling into the first filling station, I said "fill her up full with No. 1." From there on we had better power to climb up higher roads.

I can't remember where we stopped for the night, but finally we made it to Oliver around noon. Our goal was to get to Vernon before suppertime. It was in those years that highway 98 though the Okanogan Valley was a winding trail all the way from the border through to Vernon. We were thrilled at the beauty of the lakes and mountains. We were prairie chickens with flat country but I drove on and my wife commented that, by the way I drove, I had driven in mountainous terrain all my life.

It was a beautiful drive and we said "this is paradise." I want to retire here. We stopped for a moment at the Vernon lookout and headed for the church. I recall pulling up to the church and there was a group cleaning up and shining the church for our arrival. I can still see Dick Barnard polishing the brass door handles.

I can't remember who all we met but the welcome was warm and exciting. We were soon taken to our billets, which was at the motel owned by the Myrha's. These were Saskatchewan folk whom we had met before. We were to stay there until the residence would be available where we would be living for a period of time. This was the upstairs level of the home belonging to Carl and Marie Wineheimer. They lived in the suite in the basement with their son Jon. After a couple of weeks we moved into the Wineheimer home.

We soon got into the office at the church, which was located across from the rail station and flanked on one side by the Locker plant and the other by a funeral home. We used to comment that they were frozen on one side and dead on the other and we were the fire in the middle.

I will relate some of the highlights of our time in Vernon. The Sunday School was very active and with some bus ministry and contests with the Nelson church, we were able to increase our attendance to several hundred and beat Nelson several Sundays. Our services were well attended with great times of spiritual blessings and prayers. We started a radio broadcast on the local CJIB station, putting together a choir which opened the one-half hour program with "Jesus is the Joy of Living." Grace Austin at the piano and Jean Barnard at the organ, were the instrumentalists.

We called the program "Elim Fireside Hour." It was aired on Friday nights at 9:30 p.m. from the church auditorium. The choir rendered 2 or 3 numbers with a couple of specials and then a brief message. We also participated in a devotional under the auspices of the Vernon ministerial for 5 days at a time aired at 1:15 PM.

The congregation consisted of a nice group of young people—6 weddings, young marrieds and a solid group of adults. Some of the names of the good folk were Wreede, Robertson, Curtz, Marshall, Wineheimers, Myhra, Krantz, Philipchuck, Smith, Smith, Rathjen, Stanley, Boyko, Sowles, Barnard, Reimer, Michaelyk, Perchumchuk, Downs, Kowalski, Lincoln, Bulford, Rudashy, Breck, Kreise, McKay, Hunter, Writ, McDonald, Klingspohn, Sommerfeld, Sachman, Munroe, Whasiuk, Lausman, McCoy, Medinski and many other names that I cannot recall to memory. The board consisted of Pop Rathjen, Pop Renner, Bill Stanley, Dick Barnard, Mike Boyko, Norm Smith and John Michaelyk.

A major project of Elim was to construct a parsonage. A lot was purchased and John Michaelyk was the contractor. A lot of volunteer workers took part in the construction including yours truly. These bees were a great time of fun and fellowship as well as work. The ladies would provide meals so the men could work. The project was completed for some $7,000.00.

The folk were good givers and at a point when we were running low, the Austins loaned funds to the church to tide over the need. We enjoyed living in the area. There were times for picnics and swimming at Kin Beach and Kalamalka Lake. Summer was very hot and we would often take our supper to the parks. I enjoyed times of fishing and camping with the men, including some golfing.

The greatest event for us in Vernon was when our daughter Charlene was born. Grace played the piano on Sunday night then early Monday morning I took Grace to the hospital when around 8:00 a.m. Charlene was born. It was nice to have Grandma Paul with us at that time. Many in the church didn't know that Grace was expecting. We will always remember our wonderful times at Vernon and it has been one place that we have returned many, many times for holidays.

Our thanks especially to Norm and Jean Smith for their kind hospitality. Our stay was only 2 years when we were persuaded to go to British Columbia Bible Institute to assume a position of Dean of Men, Music Director and teacher. It was not easy to make this decision as we enjoyed Vernon so much and could have stayed longer. The congregation had a nice farewell with a lovely gift, and a Bible for each of the girls.

## British Columbia Bible Institute, North Vancouver, B.C.

We left Vernon in August 1956 and moved to North Vancouver, locating in a large house on St Mary's Street next to the office and boys dormitory building. The house was surrounded by large windows with a small bedroom next to the washroom, a large dining and living room, kitchen and a back bedroom. There was a small bedroom on the second floor. The basement had two apartments, which housed married students.

We got settled, getting some furniture we needed and setup for a study. I would have a small office in the next building. I remember while shopping for furniture on the way home along Marine Drive, it was pouring rain and we were rear-ended in an accident. School was to start on the 1st of September so we quickly had to prepare for our teaching and supervisory work.

The faculty consisted of Tom Johnstone, President; W. J. Friesen, Principal; Miss Eva Russett, Dean of Women; Art & Betty Schindel, Paul Barber, Grace Austin and myself. My responsibilities were to teach a full load of subjects such as Old Testament and New Testament Introduction, Religious Education, Music I, II, III, Public Speaking, Comparative Religions, General and Johannine Epistles and Gospels. I was also Dean of Mean, Music director and supervisor of all practical assignments.

Grace taught some 30 or more piano students as well as conducting typing classes. As Dean of Men, there were interesting times of counseling, keeping order, advising men's ministry aspirations, issuing dating permits, social standards and working with Miss Russet who was in charge of the girls. Chapel times were a blessing and we enjoyed lecturing and sharing our subjects with the classes. Choir practice included Grace at the piano and Mrs. Doris Johnstone at the organ.

Lunch time with the students and faculty were times of rich fellowship. The student body was comprised of wonderful young people to work with and enjoy mutual associations. Being the youngest faculty member, we could relate to the young generation. It was a good year with teaching, social times and keeping the fellows in line for the night times.

My hours were usually 6 a.m. to midnight and we enjoyed it. The term concluded with exams, banquets and graduation exercises. During our time at BCBI, we attended the 12th Street Church in North Vancouver, where Grace played for the services and we participated when asked. Immediately after school, we traveled with the quartet to promote the school, which included Dennis and Ed Pahl, Joe Young and Don Osborne, with Grace as pianist. Even during this term we would go out with a singing group for services in some of our churches in the Lower Mainland and even into the Interior. We took the choir to Glad Tidings in Victoria.

# Summer 1957 and Canim Lake

When we were asked to come to BCBI, we were assured of a complete calendar year employment. We were later informed, to our disappointment that, our income would end in April and not resume again until September, so we would have to care of ourselves for the summer.

This was a broken promise by the school so we had to make other plans. I don't know how many other faculty members were in the same boat, probably some of them. Thanks to Paul Barber, we had the summer looked after. He had been working on a project bidding on a job with the Federal Government to build a school on an Indian reserve at Canim Lake, near 100 Mile House.

Paul got the contract and put together a crew. In addition to Paul, were Ed Pahl, Larry Kellar, Martin Fideleck, the school cook and myself. While building the school we would be living in a log shack on the site. I was probably the least qualified to do construction, but Paul took pity on me and I did work with my limited ability in construction and sought to do everything I could to be of help.

The fellows all gave me lots of advice and I did everything from cement work, carpentry, digging a trench of about one mile for a water line, electrical, and plumbing. I think I became a good flunky. Martin did the cooking and we took turns cleaning up after meals. I remember one night as I finished washing dishes, I went outside to throw out the water and I said to myself "this is the gospel ministry."

On Sunday, we went into 100 Mile House for church. It was nice for me as my friends Bill and Marian Stanley as well as Norm and Jean Smith (old board members from Vernon) were part of the congregation. Paul made regular trips to the coast for materials and supplies.

While up north, Grace and the girls stayed in North Vancouver. She had her mother, Mrs. Mabel Paul, staying with her. One Saturday we went after work to 100 Mile House and went fishing with Norm Smith. We went to "Beaver Pond"—a small lake one mile square—and had to carry our boat for several hundred yards. The fish were plentiful. We got there about 6 PM and by 8 PM we caught 45 trout.

I took one trip with Paul to see my family and also help him get supplies. It was an interesting summer and we had great fellowship and lots of fun and laughter. We completed the project in good time, packed up and returned to school as teachers, students and the cook. This would be around July.

## 12th Street Church, North Vancouver

Upon returning we learned that Bob Mitchell had re-signed as Pastor of 12th Street and that the pastoral position was open. The board asked if I would act as interim pastor of 12th St. We accepted and enjoyed our ministry there with wonderful people. The board consisted of Bro. Roulston, Paul Barber, Gordon Millhouse, Claude Preston and Bro. Johnson. Foundations were completed on the property for a new church.

As part of pastoring, we worked with the congregation to proceed with construction. We saw the super structure built and ready for finishing on the inside. During our time at 12th they voted on different candidates. Each time the person would not receive the vote and our names were nominated. This took place four times and we felt it was too close to school beginning for us to leave them and accept a pastorate.

The board then asked if I would continue to serve as interim, which we did from Sept until January when they called Rev. Roy Fleming. So I carried both tasks of the school and church. The music preparation for assignments and graduation was a big load and Grace was a tremendous help as pianist. One of the music numbers was the introduction of the "Hallelujah Chorus" which continued on for many years at graduations.

## British Columbia Bible Institute, 1957-58

While serving 12th St. Church, we carried the school year with continued enjoyment of classes and school activities. I appreciated the class, which started with me. Many interesting relationships too numerous to recount took place. I did want to list them. Here are the Proclaimers: Daniel Anonby, Florence Bedwell, Mitchell Belobaba, Josephine Brown,

Larry Eytchason, Rose Giesbrecht, Wallace Hackett, Beulah Harnum, Anne Krahn, Donald Law, Brian Lord, William Mercer, Evelyn McNeil, Donald Osborne, Dennis Pahl, Edward Pahl, Bernice Pincosy, Francis Routley, Harold Routley, Marilyn Routley, Milford Rutherford, Edith Trask, Max Tymos, and Joseph Young.

When this class graduated there were 17 of the originals and they sent me an autographed year book which I appreciated so much. We were invited to a reunion of the class in later years.

As we proceeded in this term, it became evident that there were tensions building within the faculty. It appeared to us that our popularity with the students and living on campus was not going over with some of the teachers. None of this was due to anything we were doing or saying. We felt as we concluded later that we were the victims of jealousy. But school would be ending and knowing that the salary would be ending, we made plans for the summer.

Our schedule was completed with speaking at a youth camp in Washington, speaking at the youth camp in the Kootenays filling in for one month at Port Alberni for Guy Holmes and two weeks of meetings with Roy Sandercock at Nakusp and Gerald Morrison at Keremeos. That would eat up a good portion of May to August.

I should mention that in January I received an invitation from Brandon, Manitoba from Pastor Earl Williams if I would consider coming to Brandon. I replied that I was with the school until the end of April and suggested an interest on our part, but if they wanted to proceed, not to wait for us.

Graduation took place and we made plans to fulfill our summer schedule. That year (1958) General Conference was being held in Broadway Church on West Broadway. We attended and at the end took an afternoon to spend with Rob and Ruth Argue before they returned east. A meeting was scheduled that evening at Broadway with the College Board and faculty. I discovered that it was to discuss the faculty tensions. Grace, Rob and Ruth dropped me off at the church and I would return home later after the meeting.

The issues were brought up and I was accused of not doing any more in the school than I had to and of having too close an association with the students. To put it mildly, I was shocked beyond words. I couldn't believe the making of such an accusation, considering the load I carried and there never was any effort to cultivate popularity with the students. There was no counter by anyone on the board or teachers.

Tom Johnstone was leaving, having just been elected as General Superintendent of the PAOC. It was apparent the accusation came from the rest of the faculty, i.e. Friesen, Schindels, and Russett. Paul Barber was the next to be brought into the meeting. The thought within the group was 'what can we do with the situation.' It was at this point I rose to my feet and said, "I will help you and I hereby resign from my position on the faculty of BCBI" and walked out of the meeting. I later found out that Paul Barber also resigned from his position as Administrator.

Needless to say, I was devastated and left the church. As no one offered to give me a ride to North Vancouver; I walked across Granville Street Bridge to a bus stop on Georgia and returned home.

I think it was a day or so when I received a call from May English who was filling in at Bethel Temple, Brandon. She was phoning on behalf of the board saying that they were processing names for Pastoral candidate and dug up my letter from January. Their inquiry was whether I would still be interested in letting my name stand. I told May that as a matter of fact, I had just resigned from the school and would be willing to let my name stand. She said that they would be having a congregational meeting in a week and she would phone me the results. I indicated that I would be in meetings in Nakusp and she could contact me there.

We had a great beginning of services on the weekend. Week night was Tuesday and then Wednesday. After the service, we were having lunch at Pastor and Mrs. Sandercock's home when the phone call came from Brandon with the news that the congregation had given us a 97% call to come as their Pastor. As stated in a previous chapter, while we were in Semans we filled in at Brandon for a month, so the people knew who we were and our ministry.

We felt strongly that it was God's clear direction for us. We accepted and the agreement was made at that moment we would be there for the first of July. You can imagine what we were faced with. On completing the meetings in Nakusp, we returned home and immediately contacted the camps at Port Alberni and Keremeos that we regretted to have to cancel those commitments and gave the reason. The responses were very understanding and they accepted our regrets and apology.

The next thing was to complete preparations for moving. It was providential that Rev. Harold Pendray was moving to North Vancouver to be the District Director of Sunday School and Youth. Harold and his wife came over and bought most of our furniture, and Ed Paul purchased some for his folk, so we only had to pack our personal belongings.

We made our departure from North Vancouver heading for Calgary where we would stop to see David and Eleanor, Grace's brother and wife. We would also see Mrs. Paul (Grace's mother) who was living in Calgary. She later moved to Brandon to be with us.

Traveling east along Highway #1 was the usual journey. Our thoughts and conversation were filled with anticipation of our arrival and what we could face. We called to remembrance our time of filling in and meeting again with folk we already knew and it would be close to our original beginnings and would be serving family and friends.

We arrived in Brandon a few days before the first Sunday of July and moved into the parsonage at 612-14th Street that was well furnished. May English arranged to hold together the choir, orchestra and all the people for our first Sunday. Usually that was the first day of Manhattan Beach Camp when most would be at camp.

It was a great day. The welcome was wonderful and thus we began what were to be 8 ½ years of beautiful ministry to a wonderful congregation and the people of the Great Wheat City of Manitoba and its surrounding area. We will always recall our time in Brandon as one of the highlights of our ministry. It was an honor to follow seven outstanding pastors who preceded me. In retrospect, it was a very busy but blessed time with rewarding results and satisfied feelings.

The church was located at Lorne and Ninth in the center of the city. Just a couple of blocks brought you into the Main Street and the shopping area. Since our prior ministry in Brandon, expansions had occurred and there were new shopping malls, and the residential areas had spread.

Bethel Temple Church had an auditorium seating around 400 to 500 people. The lower auditorium had Sunday school classes and a small auditorium space and washrooms. The educational unit attached to the main church was an upper floor, which included the prayer room, offices and Sunday school rooms. The lower floor held an auditorium, Sunday school classrooms, kitchen facilities and washrooms. The congregation numbered around 400 and the Sunday school ran around 525.

The church had a real Sunday school program with bus ministry headed by John Hersey. It was always exciting to see hundreds of children coming by buses and cars. Mr. Ed Watt was Superintendent, Wally Cameron, the Secretary-Treasurer and we had a teaching staff second to none. Leadership before our coming had done a wonderful job of outreach in the city and community. To accommodate the crowd, we had two Sunday school Christmas Concerts every year.

The church had a weekly broadcast called "The Gospel Half Hour" on the local CJIB station. During our time there we were able to have a second release of our broadcast over the Dauphin station. We received a good mail response with donations in support of the program. Each Thursday we assembled the radio choir and specials and pre-taped the program. The format was choir numbers, special solos and duets (my wife and I), and I even played saxophone solos. I gave a brief gospel message. Grace was the pianist, Louise Shelvey the organist and Charlie Braun did the recording.

The musical program of the church was great with choir, orchestra, children's choir, special vocals and instrumentals. I will always remember Selby and Emma Smith with their violin duets. She wore glasses and he did not, but when they played, she took hers off and he put his on. Between Phil Hall and myself we led the orchestra and I led the choir. We had various special speakers and meetings that the congregation enjoyed and it was a great outreach for the church.

Every year the city had a big parade in which we decorated our bus, advertising our Sunday school. Also, once a year the City Council and Mayor would attend our morning service. Who would forget Mayor McNacca, an old army soldier?

Because of the influence of our member George Tyreman who was the Deputy Chief of Police, we would have a police group attend our morning service once a year.

A project that we completed was the renovation of the original basement and the construction of a completely new entrance. The various members of the church board were great to work with, such as Ed Watt, Clarence Lang, Art Johnston, Charlie Donagh, Charlie Sanderson, Wally Cameron, Selby Smith, Charlie Braun, Percy Shelvey, Frank Beswitherick, Benson Berry and Cliff Sampson.

We also were able to purchase a new parsonage and move from 612-14th Street to 53 Clement Drive. Brandon days were always rich times of spiritual and social activities, Christmas Board dinners, youth banquets, and Sunday School picnics. There was a wonderful group of young people. We had 33 weddings, many baby dedications and a host of funerals. We enjoyed some recreational activities such as golfing, fishing, and water skiing.

During our time in Brandon, we were part of the City Ministerial Association, both as its president and past president. An unusual experience for me was to dedicate the newly constructed 18th Street Bridge. I could hardly pray that the bridge would be a 'good boy'.

In addition to our pastoral responsibility, we were members of the District Executive over all our churches, active as Presbyter and Assistant District Superintendent. This involved many meetings, conferences and district business. We also served as president of the district Manhattan Beach Camp, 50 miles from Brandon. As part of being on the District Executive,

I was also a member of our Central Bible College Board of Governors in Saskatoon.

It was while we were in Brandon when we got word that Grace's sister Ruth had finally succumbed to cancer, which she had battled for a long time. We made plans and flew to Montreal arriving there on a Saturday. As was the Eastern custom, we joined in the viewing on Saturday, went to church on Sunday morning and back to viewing for the rest of Sunday.

The funeral service took place at Evangel Church where Rob and Ruth were the pastors. It was a beautiful service of tribute to Ruth and her outstanding Christian example and influence on many people. We stayed until Wednesday when I returned to Brandon and Grace stayed till Friday when she returned with Rob who was coming to Winnipeg. I picked up Grace and we drove back to Brandon.

It never rains but it pours. Sunday evening after church we were invited out for coffee and shortly after we arrived home the telephone rang. It was Eleanor from Red Deer informing us that David (Grace's brother) had just died of a heart attack. It was a shock to say the least. Grace lost her sister and brother within 9 days. Eleanor suggested strongly that Grace not come for the funeral, having just lost Ruth. This was appreciated. God gave us great comfort at that time. This left Grace and her aged mother who was in a rest home in Brandon. The day came when we would journey from Ontario to the funeral of Mabel Paul.

It was nice to be in Brandon during those years as we were then able to frequently visit my mother and the family in Winnipeg and Russell where I grew up and have them come to visit us. Grace was able to renew Winnipeg days, Calvary Temple and relatives in Neepawa and Gladstone.

There comes a time in one's ministry when you feel perhaps you have made your contribution to a given assembly and feel open to a change should it happen to come. Such came when a mailing came from Kitchener, Ontario in what appeared to be business material. Grace indicated that the mailing envelope was on the table but thought it was just advertising and didn't bother to open it.

As is my custom, I look at whatever comes in the mail. The envelope contained a lot of church material and a letter written by Mr. Roy Spaetzel. The envelope was from Spae-Naur Products and Roy was the president but also a board member of the Kitchener Pentecostal Assembly. I showed it to Grace and said "here's what was in this junk mail".

This package and letter was an invitation for us to consider being a pastoral candidate for the Pentecostal church. The material enclosed was information about the church. I had been referred to them by Rev. James Montgomery of the National office.

We had previously experienced the possibility of First Assembly in Calgary, which never materialized. We said, maybe this was the reason and we prayed and thought about this. Communications resulted in our flying to Kitchener to meet the Leadership, which we did. It was during an air strike in Canada and thus we had to fly to Minneapolis, Chicago and then to Buffalo, New York where we were met by some of the leadership and driven to Kitchener.

I was booked at the downtown Walper Hotel and told there would be someone to pick me up in the morning. I was given an itinerary of my stay in Kitchener. It was like a schedule for a V.I.P. Different individuals would take me to breakfast, then another two would take me to lunch, then back to the hotel for a short period of rest.

That evening another pair would pick me up for supper after which we would go to the church to meet the leadership. There we met 12 elders, 4 deacons, 4 stewards and 3 trustees, totaling 23 men. For the next few hours we shared a time of dialogue, questions, answers, church philosophy, vision and plans and relationship among other things. It was a most interesting and profitable time for myself as well as the leadership. There was a beautiful Christian spirit. There was never a moment of stress or undue sharing, which made me feel very comfortable with the gentlemen. There was a real sense of peace on the part of all of us as we anticipated what could be a positive outcome.

Returning to the hotel, I would be picked up by another team who would tour me around the city, the future site of a new church and various interest points. We then went for a quick lunch and back to the hotel. We would stay there for a time of reflection and prayer. I was then picked up by another team and we went to a large restaurant in some gardens, where we would dine with all of the leaders and their wives plus some other church leadership. It was a beautiful time of warm sharing after which we returned to the church where a large congregation was assembled to meet me. After some singing and introductions, I was asked to share briefly some spiritual thoughts and something of how I felt about coming to Kitchener and my vision of ministry. There was a question and answer period. There was nothing strained or tense with what we talked about and they asked regarding Grace and responded that they looked forward to meeting her. It was a warm time of fellowship and refreshments.

We concluded our time consenting to let our names be considered at a congregation meeting already announced. Another team drove us back to Buffalo for a midnight flight to Chicago where we would stop for the rest of the night to catch a plane in the morning for Minneapolis and Winnipeg. Upon arrival back home I spent a long time reciting all the events and observations of my trip. We would now await the call from the East. I remember the reactions of my wife when I described the classy people, ladies with stoles, etc.

After prayer and openness that this would be God's will, we felt a peace and did some research as to where we might be going. I remember some time back saying I really never want to go to Eastern Canada or United States. So much for saying "never", but it was yet to possibly happen.

Our trip to Kitchener was totally unknown to my Brandon congregation since our absence was from Monday to Wednesday.

Carrying on our task we prayed that God would direct that His will be done. This would be a major move. We loved our congregation and had no reason whatsoever to move, knowing the respect and appreciation of our wonderful people. Then Cheryl and Charlene would have to change schools. Ontario had grade 13. Music for the girls was important, grandma would have to be left behind, and Manhattan cottage would have to be sold. All these thoughts and more occupied our minds every day.

Monday was the day of voting and that evening I also had a board meeting at the church. I awaited a call from Grace while doing the business of the church. Finally the phone rang and Grace informed me that we had received a 90% vote to come as pastors to Kitchener, Ontario.

There was nothing else to do but inform the Board that we would be resigning from Bethel and that we would conclude at the end of December. This was now going on to October. To say the least, the Board was shocked and I really can't remember the conclusions at that meeting except that they were regretfully anticipating my resignation and farewell.

It was on Sunday morning and there was a beautiful spirit. However, there was a strained relationship on the part of two families and we were bringing reconciliation and forgiveness during the morning service. I remember one of our older ladies standing up and saying "don't know what this is all about, I sure feel the Lord's blessing and presence – it's wonderful."

I ministered the Word and prepared to read my resignation. I found out later that one of our prominent spiritual women said to her husband "he's going to resign". It was at that moment that I read my resignation.

The congregation was stunned and I can't recall all the reactions and comments that took place that day and in the days following. Then began the process of pastoral search. I can't recall the various names that were considered with District consultation. After numbers of board meetings, telephone calls, contacts of references etc., Rev. Wilfred Irvine was to be the candidate.

I recall one Sunday evening at Selby Smith's home, a quick board meeting was held when it was brought to our attention that Bro. Irvine had had a heart attack. I was asked to ascertain the facts. I called Rev. Irvine and asked about the matter and he responded that "a man has a right to be sick " and he said he was fine. The congregation ultimately called him as Pastor. My assistants Dwight and Anita Dobson would stay on staff and serve until his arrival.

We bid our farewell in a congregational gathering when they presented us with a beautiful mantle clock, a love offering and good wishes and prayers. Expressions of love and appreciation were overwhelming giving us a real sense of satisfaction that we served the people well. The church was left in a healthy state, finances in all funds were strong, there was no debt on the church and the church remained strong and greatly respected in the city. Thus came an end to eight wonderful years with wonderful people and memories that will always remain. The Brandon stay will be etched deeply in our remembrance with many enjoyable experiences leaving a great feeling of fulfillment. We have had the privilege of returning for anniversaries and continue to still keep in touch with some wonderful friends.

We left Brandon right after Christmas and began our journey east. Our things were on the way with the moving van and our car was loaded with our personal things and our two wonderful girls Cheryl, Charlene and our little Chihuahua, Tiny. It was not easy to uproot our kids from their friends and school but they were real stalwart bricks.

We traveled on No. 1 to Winnipeg, then Kenora, through Thunder Bay (Port Arthur and Fort William) Nipigon, White River, Sault Ste Marie, Sudbury, Barrie, Toronto and finally arrived at Kitchener on New Years Day. The journey went very well, considering that we were traveling in the wintertime, albeit the weather was great.

Upon arrival we made contact with Jack and Grace Biemen. They extended a warm welcome and kind hospitality. We would be living at the parsonage—50 Fife Avenue. Our things arrived shortly and we settled and prepared to take charge of our new pastorate. The church was located downtown on Benton Street and was a beautiful, well-built structure seating about 300 to 400 with an annex (McKenzie King's birthplace) which was connected to the main church from the basement by an underground tunnel.

The house was used for Sunday school rooms, with the 3rd floor the Prophet's chamber where missionaries or guest ministries would stay. On either side of the platform were rooms. Inasmuch as I usually had an office in the church, one of the rooms was rearranged for this purpose. It had not been used for many years, as previous pastors had their office and study in their home.

It was quite an experience to get the room ready. I remember we were taking down the old curtains and discovered they were loaded with dust and practically rotten. The custodian, Dave Martin, was so kind to help us get settled.

I can't recall much of the details of the first services. The congregation welcomed us warmly. Musically, Pauline and Jane Hamel were the pianist and organist and their father Paul Hamel led the orchestra. Our induction service was conducted on January 8, 1962. My predecessor, Rev. George Griffin, and Rev. C.H. Stiller, from the National Office officiated. As a little side, note I knew Bro. Stiller when I was a boy back in Manitoba and Marchwell, Sask. This was even before he was married. When I started ministry after graduation, he was my second District Superintendent in Saskatchewan.

On January 13 the congregation had a beautiful reception. The next days and weeks were spent with many persons. We met with the leadership, board and development committee, laying plans for a new parsonage and a new church building program. The congregation had purchased a large piece of property on the north eastern part of the city at Ottawa Street and River Road, with the idea that at some future date they would have a branch church or even relocate.

The Benton Street church was a sturdy building. It was well constructed under the leadership of a previous pastor—W. Draffin. But with changing times and modern travel, parking at the church had less than a dozen parking spots and little street parking.

We encouraged the board and congregation to move forward. Their response was enthusiastically affirmative. The building committee was made up of exceptionally qualified board members and other lay people.

The first project was the erection of a new parsonage on part of the new property. The general contractor was Elmer Evers. A lovely two-story manse was first erected. We were able to move into it on July 24 upon selling the 60 Fife Avenue residence. On September 18 we had an Open House for the congregation and some 150 came to see their new parsonage.

During this first year and into the next, many meetings were held on the agenda of building the new church facilities. One of the major considerations and plans was for the financing of the church project. We were able to approve the financing through our National Office, passing the necessary congregational resolutions.

We engaged the services of Krushen & Daily, Architects and Developers. Much time and thought went into plans and drawings for the new church. I was able to give a great deal of input into what was needed so that we would have adequate facilities to serve the ministry of the church in the city.

We wanted necessary areas and equipment that would serve young and old with our spiritual ministry. We also wanted to be an outreach church for the whole city to meet the needs of its citizens. It would be a spiritual beacon for souls to find peace and reality as can only be found in Jesus Christ. The prayers and vision of us all was that we might bless people and extend the Kingdom of God.

Finally, on January 1968 the Trustees and Board signed the deeds and mortgage for the church in lawyer Smyth's office. Bids were invited and by February 27, proposals were no longer accepted. On February 28 proposals were opened in the Spaenaur offices. The William Wolf Construction Company was awarded the contract and began the work on the grounds adjacent to our newly constructed parsonage.

While this was all in progress, pastoral duties of visitation, TV ministry, speaking engagements elsewhere, special meetings, weddings, funerals, and the launching of the first Singing Christmas Tree were our busy ministry. I recall that it was in September of that first year, our friend Mac McLeod, who was coming to visit us from Ottawa, was instantly killed in an accident on that journey.

During the stretch when the church facility was being built, we continued meeting at the Benton Street location. In the meantime, it was put up for sale by the Jack Bieman real estate company. By April offers came in and on May 22, at a congregational meeting, approval and acceptance of an offer was made to sell the property to then Kitchener Waterloo Art Gallery. Papers were signed on July 17 and our concluding Sunday in the old church was on August 11, 1968.

I remember those moving days. The first component of the new church that was built was the gymnasium. It was here that we were able to store the furniture, instruments and other items from the old church. I recall the last day when the old church auditoriums were emptied and we were cleaning up the place. Bro. Martin was at work pushing dirt and other debris with his push broom. I came along side and he stopped, looked at me with tears rolling down his cheeks.

Bro. Martin had looked after the church for many years, with meticulous care and the sanctuary looked like a spiritual palace. The House of God was David's pride and joy. Its care taking was his ministry as unto the Lord. We engaged in a few moments of conversation and he began to recount the times of spiritual blessing and moves of God. "Now" he said, "this is an empty shell". He was recounting a long history of spiritual results and hundreds of people that were reached by the ministry of the church.

We got to hear and record great events of such times when we would be part of future anniversary celebrations. I encouraged Bro. Martin with thanks for the tremendous contribution together he and his wife had made. We agreed that, though we were leaving many memories in the old building, we were taking God's Spirit and blessing into our new church building. Bro. Martin served us well. He continued as one of our Elders in our new church facility until his home-going some years later.

In the interim period, we met for services in Eastwood Collegiate until we could relocate our church services in the new gym while the rest of the construction was completed.

The building superintendent was a delightful man whose name was Jim Raikbrandt. Living next door, I often would walk over to observe the construction in progress. In speaking with Jim I would often ask questions and on a couple of occasions make constructive comments. He would say to me "I thought you were a preacher how come you know so much about construction." I didn't let on that I actually knew precious little, but with my limited knowledge, the building committee suggested I keep watch nevertheless. Jim and I had many laughs and whenever I came on the project, he would greet me with "Hi boss."

It was most thrilling to see the building project taking shape. The great beams coming together in our hexagon shaped auditorium and Sunday school annex with big cranes, was an inspiration to myself and the congregation as we anticipated a new church facility.

There was the gym, kitchen, Sunday School auditorium and class rooms, the music room, the prayer room, the choir and orchestra stands, the baptismal tank above the platform, with adjacent rooms on the second floor. On the second floor there was a one-bedroom apartment for a resident custodian. Off the foyer at the front were the offices and library. A canopy at the entrance provided for the discharge of passengers.

There was some parking at the front and a large parking lot at the rear of the property. Soon the whole project would be completed and an official opening would follow.

The day arrived November 24, 1967. Kitchener Gospel Temple, 15 Conway Drive, Kitchener, Ontario, was officially opened and dedicated. We had Open House on Saturday, November 23 for people to tour the facility. The Sunday morning service was a time of worship and rejoicing preceded by Sunday Christian Education classes.

Our official guest speaker and outstanding vocal soloist was Rev. Eddie Menaldino of Philadelphia, PA. He was a special friend of ours with whom we had been associated for many years. He had ministry with us in our church, district, and camp meeting.

The official dedication took place at 2:00 pm on November 24, 1968. Our special guests with the Pastors, Elders and official Board, were the architects, the general contractor and Dr. A.E. Bailey, President of the K/W Council of Churches; Mayor S. McLennan of the City of Kitchener; K. Hymmen, member of Parliament in Ottawa; J. Breithaupt, member of the Provincial Parliament of Ontario; Rev. Tom Johnstone, General Superintendent of the Pentecostal Assemblies of Canada; Rev. Donald Emmons, District Superintendent of Western Ontario; Rev. C.H. Stiller, General Secretary of the PAOC; and Rev. James Montgomery from the National Office.

There were many visitors from the city, surrounding areas and city churches. My assistant Mr. Gordon Bjorgan directed the special music and choir and Mr. Paul Hamel directed the orchestra.

Prior to the main service there was the laying of the 1927 corner stone by Elders, Mr. John Swartzentruber, Mr. James

Black, Mr. Lincoln Stroh and Emmanuel Swartzentruber and Deacons, Mr. John Allison Vice-Chairman and Mr. Percy Shoemaker, and Mr. Ray Bott and Mr. Leslie Winger. Then there was the laying of the 1968 corner stone by myself and Stewards Mr. Roy Spaetzel, Secretary; Mr. Donald Higgins, Treasurer; Mr. Melvin Harmer and Mr. Donald Shantz.

Behind these stones a metal box containing much memorabilia and legal papers was placed in remembrance of the official opening with Rev. C.H. Stiller offering a prayer of dedication. Additional members of the Building Committee were Jack Bieman, Mel Code and Carl Nowak. The congregation sang the doxology as we entered the sanctuary.

The service commenced with a processional of the choir and platform guests. After singing "O Canada", Rev. James Montgomery gave the invocation. The keys to the new church were presented by the Architects and General Contractor to our Trustees, Howard Hessenaur, Vernon Ramsyer and Stan Higgins. Following special music, guests, greetings, and the dedicatory message by Rev. E. Menaldino; Rev. D.A. Emmons District Superintendent conducted the act of dedication together with the congregation followed by a dedication prayer by Rev. Tom Johnstone, General Superintendent. The service concluded with the singing of "We have a story to tell to the Nations." It was a great day of celebration with the very evident presence of God.

Monday, November 25, a District Rally was held with the music and message ministry of Rev. E. Menaldino.

I purposely detailed the coming to Kitchener and the construction of the new church because in retrospect it was the most memorable and honored time of our ministry. This is not to take away from our other places of ministry and as I continue to record these, it will be with equal emotion and gratitude.

Continuing to relate our years of ministry in Kitchener, our District participation and highlights of association with a fabulous congregation of people is because we will always cherish the memories of our time in Eastern Canada.

In our time of ministry at Kitchener Gospel Temple we saw spiritual blessings beyond our deserving. We saw the church increase in conversions and miracle workings of God.

It was inspiring to preach to the people. The receptivity was so evident as people hungered for bible preaching and genuine moves of the Holy Spirit.

People prayed, ministered, sang, worshipped and gave liberally of their means and themselves to make an impact on the city and to world missions. From the youngest to the oldest we experienced solid spiritual growth. The Sunday school and bus ministry, the youth programs, the boys and girls clubs, the musicians and singers, the leaders and workers were all examples of soldiers of the cross. The standard of conduct, faithfulness, integrity, Christian lives, dedication and unstinting service made our task as pastor so peacefully free from constraint.

Our pastoral activities at Kitchener Gospel Temple included many calls to the church members. There were over 200 funerals in this older congregation, 42 weddings, many baptisms and baby dedications. I recruited and directed a great choir and under the direction of Paul Hamel, we had an orchestra, which was like a symphony, playing outstanding music. It was where Cheryl played the saxophone and Charlene played her violin. Highlights of our choir and orchestra were being invited to present music at Braeside Camp and at the Pentecostal Assemblies of North America Congress in Toronto on October 31, 1972.

While in Kitchener, we took regular holidays journeying several times to Manitoba and BC. We had a 16 foot trailer, which we domiciled at Grand Bend on Lake Huron. We spent days off and full holiday time swimming and golfing at this location. We also enjoyed holidays in Florida, USA.

We made three journeys to Winnipeg. On March 6. 1969, we visited my mother there in hospital. We returned home, but had to return the next week, for on March 10, my mother passed away. We had a service in Winnipeg on March 13 and another in Russell on March 14 with Rev. H.H. Barber officiating at her burial.

On May 30, 1971, my brother Danny passed away in Winnipeg, following which we attended his funeral. We made a fourth flight to Winnipeg for the funeral of Grace's mother, Mabel Paul. Her funeral was held November 30, 1971. We had previously made all the arrangements before leaving

Brandon, where she resided in a Care Home for several years.

Grandma was the last of Grace's immediate family. Her sister and brother had passed away during our pastoral tenure in Brandon.

While pastoring in Kitchener we celebrated the 60th anniversary of the founding of the church. This was on June 6-8, 1969. We invited all the previous pastors to participate. Of the 14 pastors prior to our time, 8 had gone to be with the Lord, but 6 were in attendance and participated in a great time of celebration.

While still the pastor, we had another celebration—65 years of ministry for the Kitchener assembly. Once again previous pastors all participated for a great time of thanksgiving for God's blessing. One highlight of this celebration was the publication of the history of Kitchener Gospel Temple by Mr. Roy Spaetzel. He was a prolific writer and provided by my request a booklet of 47 pages. It was a remarkable piece of historical writing.

This congregation continues to have an outstanding appreciation and acknowledgment of the leadership of previous pastors. My wife and I felt greatly honored by the pastors and congregation to be invited to the 70th anniversary to share in the speaking schedule.

Again, we were invited to the 75th anniversary and ministered together with former pastors. In 1990 we were again invited on the occasion and celebration and dedication of the expanded facility of the church building where we ministered in the morning service and participated in the dedication in the afternoon.

During the PAOC General Conference in 1994, we were invited by Pastor Ken Bombay to come for a Sunday evening service. We stayed with Don and Emmy Shantz. Again, we were invited to celebrate the 90th anniversary of KG in 1999. We spoke at the Sunday morning service and had a rally on Monday night. It was a great time of fellowship in the church and we appreciated the hospitality of Pastor Ken Bombay.

We also enjoyed beautiful times of social fellowship. There were great times with the Biemen, Wenzles, Ramseyers, Fincks, Cressmens, and with Don and Miriam Higgins going to the Stratford festival every year or with Howard and Marjorie Hessaneur water skiing, golfing, and cruising on the Trent canal. The hospitality of the Spaetzel's, Harmers, Howard and Carol Ramseyer, Musselmans, Martins, Schwintz, Shantz, Weilers, Strohs, Steinmans, Zehrs, just to name a few, was wonderful. There were many more—too many to list them all.

The people of Waterloo County, which included the two cities of Kitchener and Waterloo, had a profound character. It was influenced by the old order of Amish Mennonites who came from Pennsylvania in the early 1900's. The first name of the city was Berlin, but was changed to Kitchener during World War I to calm the spirit of hostility.

The cities promoted high culture and music with two universities. These were a centre of prestige and class. Kitchener's theme was "keep Kitchener as clean as a kitchen". One could not find any slum area or houses in the twin cities of 130,000 population. We often said we were privileged to live in the nicest part of Ontario.

One of our activities was to be part of the K/W Ministerial Association. Two segments of our participation was in the television ministry where we could share the message of Christ and the other segment was to be part of K/W hospital chaplaincy where we could minister to the spiritual needs of patients as part of the medical services of the hospital. The administration recognized the vital therapeutic need of counsel and prayer of the clergy.

During our time I was involved by being elected by the District Executive of Western Ontario. We served with Superintendents D. Emmons and H. Honsinger and members Larry Talbot, William Moody, Ted Adams, Ray Stewart, Ron Stevens, John Richardson, Victor Brown, Homer Cantelon, and Jack Counsel.

These were times of enjoying fellowship with the members and with all the District Conferences and workers. I appreciated the confidence to be elected for most of our years in Ontario, being the new kid on the block as it were. We had a part in the erection of the Auditorium at Braeside Camp; sitting on the Board of Governors of the Bible College in Peterboro; and serving on District and National committees. I was asked to speak at district rallies and other church events. We served on the Board of Crossroads television programs of David Mainse. While in Ontario we were able to take time to visit eastern Canada. There was Expo 67 in Montreal, and conferences in Halifax, which gave us all the opportunity to travel in the Eastern United States; New Brunswick Cabot Trail, and returning to Quebec City. We saw many interesting sites and magnificent beauty. On our trip to Halifax, Charlene and her friend, Charlotte Cressman, made our trip very memorable. It certainly was a picture of old Canada compared to the west.

We had opportunity to visit places in Ontario. One such occasion was to travel on Eric McLean's boat to One Thousand Islands. We saw many places in Toronto. Visits to the Harmer Cottage and the Ramseyer cottage in the Muskoka's and Kawarthas. When friends visited us we would often travel to Niagara Falls.

Waterloo county was the Amish Mennonite country. There we saw beautiful farm buildings all painted clean. One would pass many horses and buggies on the roadways. St. Jacobs was a most interesting place with its shops laden with crafts and produce of the rich farming area. Elmira was a place where we visited many times.

We had occasion to attend a service in an Amish Mennonite church. As we arrived there would be as many as 300 horses and buggies tied up around the building. The church was a simple rectangular building with seating along one side facing the pulpit which was located to the opposite side and there was seating at both ends facing toward the centre pulpit. It was interesting to see the order of seating. At one end seating was for the single men and the other end for the single girls. The side seating was for the married couples. You can draw your own conclusion as to the reason.

The service was conducted by laymen, insofar as they do not have paid clergy. There were three speakers, which resulted in a three-hour service. The service was inspiring and sincere in its exultation of the Lord Jesus Christ. We thoroughly enjoyed the experience

The Amish folk have unique vocabulary of expressions. Some examples are: "Aunt Emmy's, "she don't feel so pretty good" or "Yonnie stung his foot with a bee and it ouches him terrible" or "Amos and Becky live the hill a little up, out where the road gets all" or "the speck and beans is all up, but the schnitz un knepp is yet" or "Amos came from the yard in mom's on the table and the pops have et already" or "when Salom marries Sammy she'll be fixed off good aint" and I think this one is cute – "I'd like to get went with…but boys aint so much for me".

To have had the opportunity and honor to live in Ontario and see Eastern Canada and be a part of the people there—particularly our very own church congregation—was an experience both Grace and I shall long remember. During this period of time, our girls were able to complete their school grades.

Cheryl took a job as secretary to a Bank Manager and later worked for a Television company. Charlene, while yet in school, started as a cashier at Zellers store. She also was a volunteer candy striper in the hospital, experiencing her first exposures to a nursing career.

We had started in Kitchener January 1, 1967 and it was close to the end of 1974. Everything was going great and we were happy in our ministry. Cheryl was employed at the TV station and Charlene was registered to begin nurses training at Kitchener's Continental College.

September 3 was going to be our 25th wedding anniversary. We loved our church family and looked forward to expanding our ministry. What I am about to relate was not in any way anticipated or even dreamed of. It was the year of General Conference, which was to be held in Regina, Saskatchewan in August.

Our plans were to motor to the areas of our beginnings. We traveled all the way back to Vernon where we had had a pastoral ministry. It was there we would visit with our friends—the Norm and Jean Smith family.

En route we visited family in Winnipeg, Russell and Calgary. We arrived in Vernon and pulled up to our friend's home where we would be received with a very warm welcome. It was so good to see them. The anticipation of a wonderful visit would now be fulfilled.

It wasn't but a few minutes when Jean said there is a phone call waiting for me from Kamloops. My heart sank, for I suspected what it might be about. I knew that Calvary Temple in Kamloops was looking for a pastor. There were people in that congregation who were part of my congregation in Brandon. Maybe it was a call to just say hello but maybe not.

Returning the call, I spoke with Cal Cresswell who was phoning on behalf of the Board, asking if we would consider coming to Kamloops and meet the Board. To this day I do not know how they knew I was in the area. We decided that after our visit in Vernon we would journey by Kamloops on our way back to the Regina conference and then back to our Kitchener pastorate.

Without relating the details here, we had been asked several times to come to Kamloops to assist Rev. Gaglardi. We had been with him at other times, but never felt we wanted to get involved as far as pastoring was concerned.

After our time in Vernon we traveled on to Kamloops to see old friends and meet with the church board. They requested that we let our names be considered for the pastorate. During the next hours and days we really had to analyze and pray about the matter. As I have indicated in this chapter there were the girls to consider. In particular, Charlene was registered in the Nurses College in Kitchener and was to begin her studies and training in a matter of a days.

We felt we should inquire at Cariboo College and Royal Inland Hospital to determine the possibilities for her nurse training in Kamloops. Also, what would be involved for her admission, and when her studies would begin. The girls were shocked when we contacted them. We deferred discussion of the details until we got home. There was some course difference from Ontario that would have to be sorted out.

We toured the church and after more meetings with the Board, we assessed the matter. We decided to allow our names to stand on the condition that our concerns in relation to Charlene could be satisfied. We felt if it was not to materialize, we would accept it as God's will because there was no reason for us to leave our present pastoral charge. We knew the feelings of various members of the congregation in Kitchener, who made it known to us that we could remain there for the rest of our ministry. These were kind, sincere words, which we appreciated.

After Conference was over, we returned to Kitchener, hardly knowing what would happen and what was planned by our girls. They had taken it upon themselves to have a 25th wedding anniversary celebration for us. The congregation had been invited and all preparations were made to have an Open House at our home.

They had worked on the food program and the works. What a beautiful surprise, we were so proud of our girls. All the folk brought many gifts and good wishes. It was a total success and will always be grateful to the people for their generous spirit. The church gave us a silver cutlery chest, which we will always cherish.

Now we waited what would happen as far as Kamloops was concerned. We knew the date of their meeting and we had learned about Charlene's passing the Nursing School's requirements, etc. Well, it happened. The same day that the vote was to be taken in Kamloops, Cariboo College phoned to say that Charlene was accepted for nurses training, including transfer of credits.

At 11:00 p.m. that same evening, we received a call from the Kamloops congregation with a 96% vote. Thus the stage was set for our departure back to British Columbia. The classes for Charlene had started the first of September and we would not be able to leave until October. It became necessary for Charlene to go on to Kamloops before us. We bid her farewell at the Toronto Airport the next morning. We had called our friends Murray and Marilyn Thomson and asked if she could stay with them. They were very delighted to have her.

We made preparations for leaving Kitchener. We tendered our resignation and made arrangements for Cheryl, who for the present, would remain behind because she was working. Our announcement to the congregation shocked everyone. They wanted to know why we were leaving. It was difficult to do especially when they had been so generous and supportive in every way. We could only believe that it was God's leading. Not understanding it all, we prayed that God would continue to guide us as well as the Kitchener church's future.

There were various gatherings connected with our farewell by the church. We also had a variety of pastoral items to tidy up. We gave whatever counsel we could to the leadership in their search for a new pastor prior to our farewell Sunday. The days were filled with packing for the move and arrangements for the movers. We would be loading our car as well as our 16 foot trailer with personal things, plants, and our little dog Tiny. It was during about the third week of October we started our journey for B.C.

We decided that we would take the American side going through Sarnia, the Makinak bridge and come back into Canada at Emerson, Manitoba. We had some dramatic experiences with our plants and our dog. But God, through it all, granted us safe passage back into Canada, having been told that we might have problems. At stops along the way, we carried our plants into our motel room because of an overnight frost possibility. The journey was safe and were able to get to Winnipeg and then on to Saskatchewan, Alberta and finally Kamloops.

I cannot close this chapter without expressing the deep feeling my family had for the opportunity of our Eastern Canada sojourn. Eastern people revealed a character quite unlike that of the old west. Apart from the tensions that are often expressed about the East having no heart for the West, the people in general were hospitable, wholesome and loving. This was especially true of the folk of our church and the people in the community. I feel that we have received great personal value that has enriched our lives and broadened our concepts. We are the better for it especially the spiritual nutritive that made our lives much broader than it would have been. Thanks be unto God who led us through this Eastern journey.

## Kamloops, British Columbia

Kamloops was not new to us. We had been there while pastoring in Vernon and attended a great opening of the church when R.J. LeTourneau was the dedication speaker and Rev. Phil Gaglardi the pastor. I had several invitations to come on staff by Mr. Gaglardi. Now, many years later, we found ourselves becoming the Pastor.

We arrived in Kamloops around October 20 and moved into the parsonage at 510 Grandview Terrace. A congregational welcome with groceries was held on October 30. Our first services were on November 30. Our introduction was a bit of a culture shock, especially after Kitchener. Knowing some folk from previous times and added to them, members of the Board, we soon came to know some wonderful people. And so began our pastoral ministry in Kamloops.

It was so nice to have Charlene back with us and see her deeply involved with real enjoyment in her studies at Cariboo College and Royal Inland Hospital. In our previous chapter we mentioned that Charlene had been registered to train in Kitchener and would face all the costs. Now at Kamloops she discovered that the BC Government had launched a program to provide full tuition and a monthly allowance, due to a shortage of nurses,. So Charlene was able to receive her RN in two years. It made our move more comforting, and we thank the Lord for His provision.

After we arrived, the Board proposed that we consider owning our own home. Up to this time in our ministry we lived in church parsonages. This was the housing provided as part of our salary and precluded us being able to accumulate any assets. They offered to sell the parsonage on Grandview Terrace. Financing was arranged and title to the property was transferred to us. Housing allowance was paid to us whereby, with a down payment, we could obtain the necessary mortgage. This was greatly appreciated and now for the first time in our lives we owned property. We had to do some renovations, which included new carpets and drapes, etc., for a cost of $7,000.

Within a month after our arrival in Kamloops, our daughter Cheryl, who remained in Kitchener, felt she would also like to move to the West Coast. She resigned her position and Grace flew back to Kitchener to motor back with Cheryl in late spring of 1974. It was so nice to see her, but it wouldn't be for long, as she really wanted to go to Vancouver. There, she stayed with her cousin Judy until she found a job and an apartment in North Vancouver. She motored back to Kamloops every long weekend and it was so nice to be together as a family.

Our tenure in Kamloops was from October 1974 until August 1976. It was the shortest stay in any place we were pastoring. It became apparent later that this was to be when we received a call to Victoria. One of the conditions that Victoria had in calling a new pastor, was that he was to be in the B.C. District. We accepted the quick change as being God's arrangement for us.

Even in the brief period at Calvary Temple we had a busy time with various activities. There were the regular pastoral duties, visiting and pulpit ministries. Within this time we had 7 weddings, 9 baby dedications and 14 water baptisms and a few funerals.

We had a number of guest ministries such as Dave Iverson, Ken McGillvary, the Matsons, the Coraliers, Evelyn Glosser, R & D Donnelly, Bill Burkett, Kroze Bros., Yongi Cho from Korea and Rob Argue. We had visits from Jack Bieman, the Hubleys, H & C. Ramseyer, Les & Dot Winger, Don & Miriam Higgins from our previous pastorate in Kitchener. I should also mention that Phil & Jennie Gaglardi were part of the congregation. Their assistance in the Sunday school was greatly appreciated.

When they were the pastors they had built up the Sunday school to 1,000 or more. The congregation was made up of many great people and we enjoyed great fellowship working with them. People like the Thomsons, Mistals, Cresswells, Brecks, Dredgers, Strohmeirs, Goodmans, Myhres, Burns, Hartwicks, Margaret Logan (my secretary), just to name a few, were great.

The services were well attended and there was a nice group of young people during our time. There were about 15 people who chose to be part of another church being formed and we wished them God's blessing.

During our time at Kamloops we took holidays at Paul Lake in our trailer, as well as at Thomson's cottage on the Shuswap. We also attended the Basic Youth Conflicts Seminar in Seattle. In May 1976 we attended anniversary services in Brandon. We spent some days at "Gaglardi's shack" on Kamloops Lake.

A family highlight while we pastored Calvary Temple was when Charlene graduated with her RN. The graduation exercises were held in our church on July 24, 1976. It was an inspiring event.

While it was a distinct contrast to our time in Ontario, we enjoyed being back in B.C. Kamloops has its own beauty. The desert hills, the surrounding ranches and lakes, together with the city sitting at the confluence of the Thompson and Fraser rivers, represents a very picturesque scene.

It was in June 1976 that we received a call to Glad Tidings church in Victoria. The Kamloops church was shocked at our resignation from Calvary Temple, but we felt it was in God's will that we accept the call to Victoria. The congregation, however, was very understanding and gave us their blessing. We will always have many pleasant and wonderful memories spent with this famous congregation that had been pastored by the great Phil Gaglardi. We enjoyed fellowship with the Gaglardi family and many years later attended the funeral service of Phil Gaglardi in the church that he built.

## Victoria, British Columbia

It was the last weekend of May during the event "Swift Sure", which was a boat race from Victoria to Seattle, that we flew to Victoria to meet with the Board. It was agreed to let our names be voted on, which was done after the two-week requirement of the church's constitution. We received an approximate 96% vote and were scheduled to assume the pastorate with the first service on September 5.

With this in mind, we spent August preparing to leave Kamloops, searching for housing in Victoria, and packing. Through Steve Salaga, the church realtor, we were able to purchase a home on Elnido Crescent, in the Gordon Head district.

Our furniture was picked up by Bob Fleming and Bob Holden who moved us on behalf of the church and it was unloaded by men from the church, thus reducing the moving costs considerably. We were able to sell our Kamloops house on August 14 and Grace, with Charlene left for Victoria while I stayed behind to complete the house deal and then join them on the next day, August 15. In Victoria, we appreciated the hospitality of Reg and Thelma Bowering until we could get settled in our new home.

My first day in the office was September 1. Eleanor Rogers was a very helpful secretary. Our welcome service was specially arranged, that is, we were kept in the office until the service began and then we were escorted to the platform to the applause of the congregation. Thus began our ministry in Glad Tidings Church, which would be followed by almost nine years of interesting, challenging, busy, and wonderful times. The balance of 1976 was spent in pastoral activity, development committee meetings, calls, banquets and the usual year end activities. Bill Hale, who was on pastoral staff, was a great help as he looked after Christian Education, Music, and Youth.

The year of 1977 was filled with a multitude of activities. There was much preliminary work in preparations for the construction of a new church building. The church was located on North Park Street. The adjacent Catholic school had been purchased through the foresight and urging of Mr. Ernie Hudson. It was to be put to good use for Sunday school classes and youth activities. The property extended to Quadra Street, and the plans were to construct the new facility connected with the old church. We engaged Vern Delgetty as our architect. We also arranged and had approved a mortgage certificate financial program as we had done in Kitchener Ontario. We were able to quickly raise the necessary funds to sign our contracts. The National Office reinforcement followed. Before we even started, we were able to raise $300,000.00, and we then launched into plans for the building.

We had an excellent development committee of board members and representation from the congregation of both men and women. Eventually, by the middle of 1977 congregational approval enabled us to proceed with bid invitations. The contracts were signed with Campbell Construction. Work began by moving out the school buildings for demolition, followed by preparatory work to lay the foundations. I remember a walkway had to be constructed in order to enter the old church building for regular services.

The year was filled with a variety of events, e.g. a couple of weddings, a funeral, a concert with Swedish singer Karl Olivebring and special services with Bill Burkett. It was in May that we said farewell to Assistant Bill Hale who was going to the District Office in charge of Childrens Ministry. We also had a special congregational meeting to approve the sale of the Colville Branch church in Esquimalt. In this year Eleanor Rogers was married and moved up Island. Viola Smith became my secretary, and she served the church for the rest of my time in Victoria and beyond.

The year 1978 became a great year for Glad Tidings Church. While construction progressed on the new sanctuary and its facilities, our pastoral duties were filled with ministries that allowed us to become familiar with the members of the congregation, the city of Victoria and its suburbs.

One of the interesting events was the many weddings that took place. There were 14 that year. It seemed that the young people, for sentimental reasons, wanted to have their wedding in the old church. They had spent their growing up years there, so this was understandable. In our time in Glad Tidings we performed 58 weddings, which was an average of 7 per year.

It was inspiring to have such a host of young people in the church and to be able to minister not only to them but the older members as well. Statistically, over our years at Glad Tidings we baptized in water 192 people, one of which (Mark Wuerch), in later years became my son-in-law.

We dedicated 88 babies and conducted 85 funerals. Many new members were added to the church.

Coming back to this great year of 1978, it was to be an historic event in the life of the church. The building committee was busily involved in the details of what would be the new church facility. Included was a sanctuary, seating over 1100.

The unique layout provided for a glass front and platform with a centre baptismal tank, a perimeter layout for a future balcony, Sunday school classrooms, a prayer room and the administration offices. The exterior on two sides was all glass.

The new construction was beautifully connected with the old church. An interesting item in the erection of the sanctuary was the size of the laminated beams, which were constructed in Vancouver and had to be brought over by barge. They were brought to the church site during the night by special trailers when traffic would be minimal on Pat Bay Highway.

The *Times Colonist* reported that these beams were the biggest ever brought into Victoria. The exact measurements were 18" wide, 4 feet deep and 135 feet in length weighing 15 tons. They provided a sanctuary with no posts. Pews were made in Modesto, California. Bob Fleming, our building committee chairman, and myself, together with our wives traveled, to see their construction. The committee members all gave very valuable input so as to provide a facility that would serve the congregation and the city with the full message of the Gospel.

The choir was rehearsing with Gordon Krause as director. The orchestra/band was under the direction of Chrissy Denton. Our youth pastor, David Pennoyer, and the membership rallying to polish up the building and preparing refreshments in readiness for the great opening.

October 27-29 had arrived. Friday evening was our great banquet held at Garth Homer Centre, with a full attendance and inspiring celebration. Saturday was Open House and our youth guides led tours of the whole facility. Refreshments were served. Sunday morning service was a time of worship and I brought the message on "Here for a time such as this", based on the story of Queen Esther.

Sunday afternoon was the official opening and dedication. Our special guests were Mr. A. McKinnon, Member of Parliament, Mr. Barber, Member of the B.C. Legislature; the Alderman of the City of Victoria Larry Ryan; and Rev. Robert Taitinger, our General Superintendent who was the speaker for the occasion.

Rev. James House, our District Superintendent, conducted the dedication. Other guests included Rev. A. Johnson, President of the Council of Churches; Mr. H. Curtis,

MLA; Rev. R. Feltmate, President of the Pastors Fellowship; Rev. H. Pendray, our Island Presbyter; and former Pastors E.W. Robinson and Paul Hawkes. Also attending were William Campbell, our General Contractor; and our Architect Vern Delgetty. Mrs. Maisie Hornby was also a special guest, representing her husband who was one of the Pastors of Glad Tidings. Guest soprano soloist for the weekend was Mrs. Chris Hansen Monson of Seattle, Washington.

Congratulatory wires were received from former pastors and members of Glad Tidings from Agincourt and Kitchener, Ontario. The same were received from Edmonton, Alberta; Glendora, California, and churches of the B.C. District. The dedication saw the sanctuary filled to capacity with people from other churches joining in our celebrations. It will be a time I shall long remember, which gave me opportunity for the following years to minister in Glad Tidings church.

In appreciation for our leadership in the construction of the new church, members of the congregation surprised us with a gift by sending us to Hawaii for two weeks. Bob and Ruby Fleming joined us. It was a first for us all and we had a wonderful time.

During the following year we experienced steady spiritual growth in the church. Special guest ministries included Peter Yongren, Jack Duckworth and Percy Brewster of England; Canada for Christ Crusade with Roy Davis, and Rev. & Mrs. Clinton Ward Children's crusades; Swedish soloist Carl Olivebring, and Rev. James Montgomery, all contributed ministry to the congregation.

Sunday School, bus ministry, youth outreach with the District Ambassadors in Mission (A.I.M.) discipleship classes and great Sunday morning worship services and Sunday night evangelistic rallies were the spiritual thrusts of the church. My assistants during our ministry in Glad Tidings were Gordon Krause, Dave Pennoyer, Mark Hawkes, Ken Kubryn, Lester Markham, Emmanuel Jensen and Rankin McGougan (two of them at different times), most of them moved to other ministries.

Holidays were also taken to attend anniversary churches in Kitchener. We were active in the local ministerial association and served on the District Executive as Presbyter and

Assistant Superintendent. A special highlight for me was to go to the sessions of Parliament and pray before the question period. Grace was also deeply involved with Wee College, Crusader program of the boys and girls and with the Women's Ministry. After Gordon resigned, Grace conducted the choir for 4 years and did a fabulous job in Christmas and Easter presentations.

There were instances of heavy counseling and visitation to hospitals, jails, and pastoral care visits to shut-ins. Since there were many older people in the congregation, there were many funerals including some well known persons associated with our Fellowship who had retired in Victoria.

We had some very qualified members as lay persons to assist us in giving counsel to crisis situations. We saw some remarkable conversions and healings. Our altars and prayer room on Sundays were filled with young and old finding Christ in powerful experiences made real by the power of the Holy Spirit.

Another momentous year for us was 1980. On June 22, following the evening service, I suffered a mild heart attack. For some weeks I had been feeling very tired as we gave ourselves unreservedly to our pastoral duties. I guess when one is on the go more hours and days without taking some time out, it catches up with you. Charlene, our daughter in the choir, noticed me at the pulpit and commented to Grace at the piano "I think dad is having a heart attack."

We concluded the service and Charlene took me to the Jubilee Hospital where she was nursing. I was rushed past a full waiting room and the nursing station, and then transported in a wheel chair, I was soon lying down and on monitors. I was in hospital for 15 days guarded by nurses who wouldn't let anyone come visit me. Upon discharge I was at home for a week or so but continued to have chest pains.

My darling daughter went to work on a Monday morning and reported to Dr. Woodark (my cardiologist), that I was not doing so well. He immediately told Charlene to phone me and have me come in for an angiogram. It was quickly discovered I had 3 or 4 arteries blocked in the high 90's. Dr. Woodark admitted me and declared that he had a gut feeling I had to have open-heart surgery immediately. With all the preparations, getting blood supply and scheduling completed, that Friday I had quadruple bypass surgery.

After intensive care for three days, I was put in a public ward and nine days later I was home. My orders were that I couldn't go back to work for three months. My family was most caring through the whole ordeal. It was very consoling to have the nurse daughter as well as the vigilant help of my daughter Charlene and my wife Grace.

During our recuperation, I appreciated so much how Ken Kubryn and Mark Hawkes and Emmanuel Jensen took care of all the ministry of the church. The years that they were with me will be long remembered as beautiful times of friendship and working together. These were great guys and we continue to enjoy their friendship and often talk about our times at Glad Tidings.

I was back at church by September 7th for three hours each day in the office. I brought my first message on October 5th. During my time in hospital, a personal friend, Mrs. Olive Shipton, passed away. She was on the faculty of BCBI and I followed her on staff. My tenure on the staff was recorded in my previous chapter. Her niece and husband were part of my Vernon congregation.

When I returned to my pastoral duties at Glad Tidings there was no shortage of weddings (32) and funerals (26). We continued to experience inspiration and growth in the Assembly. One monthly event under the direction of Mark Hawkes called "Maranatha" youth rallies, saw capacity attendances as young people were reached with special musical groups.

In September of 1981 we decided to take a tour to the Holy Land. Our group of 10 from the church had a marvelous time. To have been in the Holy Land is an experience we shall never forget.

It was at the end of 1984 that we concluded our ministry at Glad Tidings. There was a large attendance at our farewell with numerous expressions of appreciation for our ministry. We had made our contribution to the church. Having received a call to New Westminster, we accepted and were again on the move.

# Connaught Heights Pentecostal Assembly
# New Westminster, British Columbia

It was in January 1985 that we began our pastoral ministry to this well-known congregation. It had begun in the 1930s, and had been a vibrant church. I recall when we were on staff at BCBI how many of the students loved to attend there. Some of the early pastors were there for short terms until Rev. Marvin Forseth became pastor. He came in the early 1950's and was there for almost thirty years.

We spent six and a half years at Connaught. The interesting highlights of our time there are worth recounting. Many things needed attention. The congregation, though small, responded well and we saw growth and God's blessing as we started to reorganize and improve the facility to develop ministry programs. We had an hour-long live TV program over Western cable with music, guests and ministry of the Word. We had a weekly "dial a message" so that people could phone and receive spiritual help and guidance.

Special crusades were held. The Villa Senior Citizen residence was reorganized and properly constituted with by-laws and accounting regulations. Other guest ministries and myself conducted weekly services. We were very honored to have retired ministers like Rev. & Mrs. C. Ward, Rev. & Mrs. B. Parkinson and missionaries like Nellie Hendrickson, Florence Spence, Rev. & Mrs. H. Matson, and laymen minister Steve Shabak.

Most of the residents were members of the congregation.

There were great times of spiritual and social fellowship with the Villa residents. The youth and Sunday school programs were revitalized and new contacts were made as we endeavored to reach out to the community. Pastoral Care, biblical teaching, and visitation brought new folk into the church. The music department was developed by a choir and orchestra and became an opportunity to present the Gospel in special Christmas, Easter and other events.

In our time at Connaught we received into membership 82 people, dedicated 21 infants, baptized in water 54. We conducted 31 weddings and had 58 funerals, some of which were after we had left as Pastor of the church.

I had a grand board with some of the greatest men any pastor could wish for. Men such as Roy McLean, Tom Martin, Jonas Johnson, Arnie Bjurling, Ron Collins, Ron Hammel, Joe Thomas, Stan Perwal, Peter Meister and Elders Bill Stanley, Alf Hansen, and Joe Allinger.

Our board meetings started with almost an hour of prayer and business was attended to with a real spirit of love and unity. Because of these good men we were able to make necessary changes and improvements in the church. I have always appreciated the good boards, which I had in every church.

During our time, we led the congregation in many administrative matters. When we arrived the church debt was almost one-half million dollars. We were able to reduce that amount by 75%. In addition to renovations, redecorating, and new carpeting, we installed new pews in the sanctuary. The church and office equipment was replaced. The exterior of our church building was redecorated. The congregation responded with generous finances and the accounting was revamped and solidified.

I appreciated my assistants who served with me. They were Gary and Sandra Wilson, Bruce Greenwood, Albert and Beth Shindel and Sheena Mohipp. James Raman led the East Indian Congregation of our assembly. Together we served the community. I also appreciated the laypersons that led the music, Sunday school, Youth and Women's Ministries.

I was still involved with District Executive work. A great event, which took place at this time, was the plan to have a Christian School. The Christian Education and Communication Society was organized. It included Pacific Academy.

Our sponsor was the Pattison Foundation, which provided the funding. I was asked to serve on the Board as Vice Chairman, which lasted for ten years. The school started in Coquitlam then moved to a 36-acre campus in Surrey. The school continued to increase its enrollment. Today it has a student body of 1200. Grace served in the office for around 6 years. Mark, our son-in-law, who teaches in the high school and our grandson Aaron, are part of the school to the present time. The school built a world-class facility and has become an outstanding educational success with an international outreach.

When Grace and I arrived in New Westminster, we purchased a beautiful home on Glenbrook Drive, where we lived for 4 years. Charlene had already moved over to Vancouver and was nursing in the Royal Columbia Hospital. Before she left Victoria she was courting Mark Wuerch. It didn't take long for Mark to propose, and they set their wedding date for April 12, 1986.

They were married in Broadway church with Allon Hornby taking the first part then I did the marriage ceremony. Judy played the piano. Charlene's attendants were Cheryl, Linda and Cindy. Mark's attendants were John Edgar, Alex Loosdrecht and Rod Penman. Don and Diane Liesch provided the music. Their reception was held at Robson Manor in New Westminister. They went to the Cook Islands for their honeymoon.

Shortly after we were offered a good price for our house, so we decided to move to the New Westminster Quay, living in Tiffany Shores. It was a beautiful place. In a couple of years we were offered a good price. We sold it and moved next door to the Promenade. However, it was a much smaller complex.

In June 1995 we saw a big ad in the paper advertising semi-detached homes in North Surrey. We went the next day and purchased #13 10505 1171st. We took possession in June. It continues to be our place of residence. Grace was still working at Pacific Academy just a few blocks from our new residence, which made it very convenient. To this day it has been nice for Aaron as he attends the school where Mark works and if needed, he can run over to our residence after school to wait for his dad.

In our time at Connaught Heights Church, we acquired some very lasting friendships. We have had many opportunities to return for fellowship and ministry. We received some very exciting news in December of 1990. Charlene informed us that she was pregnant and expecting her baby in August of 1991. I had already resigned from Connaught, and we left there the end of August.

The church congregation had a farewell for us. Adding to this excitement was that our grandson Aaron would be just 10 days old and dedicated by this new grandpa prior to our leaving Connaught. Everyone was so excited to see him. This completed 43 years of ministry as Pastor, College teaching and Evangelistic crusades.

It was only a matter of 7 days when we were invited to assume new types of ministry that would take us into another 11 years of what would still keep us in full time service. So, retirement was not on the schedule. Those years would prove to be the most enjoyable and fulfilling times in our lives.

# Chapter 6

## *Christian Service Never Ends*

W e scarcely had time to think about the future, when just a few days after our resignation we were invited to serve as interim pastor at the Abbotsford Pentecostal Assembly.

Mr. Bill Sharp of the church board phoned and asked if we would come and meet with the board to accept and lay plans for our leadership of the church. We felt it was the Lord's will to accept and help the assembly during this time of their pastoral search. We thought that perhaps it would be for a short period but the length turned out to be nine months.

Grace and I fully enjoyed this assignment. The board and congregation were very kind and appreciative of our ministry. The pastoral assistants and office personnel were most helpful with information and assistance. The congregation was made up of all ages and their participation in the church program was one of faithful and loyal dedication. Since the church was only recently built, the financial load was quite heavy, but the congregation responded very generously and we saw the debt reduced and the giving increased.

There were numerous Sunday school classes for all age groups of children and youth. Very qualified teachers taught many elective adult classes. The youth program during the week was very vibrant and well attended. We started a weeknight adult bible study and prayer night, which grew to an attendance over 150. There was an active senior's group meeting weekly under the direction of the seniors' pastor. The music department was excellent with choirs, specials, and instrumentals directed by the music pastor, who also led the worship services.

Many social gatherings were held on special occasions, which were serviced by very efficient catering groups. There was an elder group that held weekly prayer meetings. It was also an honor to have a number of retired ministers and missionaries as part of the congregation. The Bible College faculty and students were an excellent addition to the church in teaching and participating in many ways.

We enjoyed some special speakers for our main services and the congregation responded well and valued their ministries. The attendance of 800 people at the Sunday morning services saw the auditorium and balcony filled. The evening Gospel services saw the church well filled. The prayer room was always filled with great prayer warriors. On Sunday nights we saw great moves of the Holy Spirit with spiritual results at the altar as we concluded the service. There were many instances of counseling and prayer for situations that arose in people's lives. The church was a place where many community people would seek out spiritual help.

We can honestly say that our time at APA was a highlight in our years of ministry. The people expressed gratitude for our leadership and even after we left, they continued to say they missed us being there. We have been able to return for visits and anniversary celebrations and always enjoyed our friendships and fellowship with the people. It was a great time for us in a great church. Upon our leaving, Rev. Paul Hawkes was installed as the new pastor.

After this period of time we were invited to speak at the Seniors' Camp in Saskatchewan. We then also went to Brandon to minister in our former Bethel Temple Church. From there, we went on to visit my sister Helen in Winnipeg. On our return trip home, we also ministered in Barriere. We returned to Winnipeg as my sister was not well and had decided to relocate in a senior's complex. We assisted her in the process of selling her home and moving into her new place of Wellesly Apartments located on Portage Avenue near Grace hospital.

Upon returning home we ministered in the Port Moody Church for a Sunday and in the latter part of that year, we went on holidays for a couple of weeks at Puerto Vallarta, Mexico.

During the year 1993 we went on holidays with Norm and Jean Smith to California. It was a most enjoyable time going along the west coast through San Francisco, Los Angeles, San Diego and Capistrano. We took a drive to San Clemente, the home of Richard Nixon, where we had an encounter with some very aggressive people who, when they took a look at Norm, made a hasty retreat. Traveling via Indio, we visited Norm's brother Al. After spending some time in Palm Springs we made the return trip to our home.

We continued with our District responsibilities as Assistant District Superintendent. Conference came along and a new Superintendent was elected. This meant that time was needed for the transition and I was asked to act as Superintendent, which lasted for some two months. With an interim charge of the District Office, there were many business items related to official correspondence and attending to church needs.

We offered counsel to pastoral situations and enjoyed working with the District Secretary, Harold Pendray; as well as the office staff and the youth director David Larson. Having been involved deeply with the district affairs and knowledgeable about its history, it was helpful to me when giving counsel as the need arose. It was a very pleasant time and we appreciated the opportunity to serve the District during that short period.

Following this we attended the 45th anniversary of our college class reunion in Winnipeg, which was a great highlight as it was the first reunion we had since Graduation in 1948.

There were about 30 of the class of 35 who attended with their spouses. What a time we had! We were recognized by Pastor Barber in the Calvary Temple morning service.

When the new B.C. District Superintendent was elected he resigned his church which left a need for someone to pastor the church during their pastoral search. That is how I ended up serving as interim Pastor of the Port Moody assembly. This led to four months of looking after the church and assisting the board in its pastoral search.

Our time in Port Moody was again a most interesting and enjoyable time. The church board was a group of Christian gentlemen vitally involved and interested in the future of the church. The pastoral staff included a youth pastor, a visitation pastor and a church secretary. There was a vibrant

Sunday school with excellent teachers; a great youth group; a music ministry team with talented singers and musicians.

Adjacent to the church was a house turned into a youth centre with activities, computers, and a library, which was used to reach the youth of the community. With a regular flow of youth from the high school across the street, many attended the regular church services. The church facilities also housed a day care centre operation, reaching many boys and girls.

Our services were well attended and there was a real freedom of worship and prayer. We enjoyed ministering to a very attentive and appreciative congregation. Both Sunday morning and Sunday evening services had an attendance that filled the sanctuary. Altar services saw God moving by His Spirit as souls were saved and believers blessed. We will always remember these spiritual times of God's blessing. We felt blessed and honored in our time at Port Moody.

Prior to our coming there, plans had been initiated for relocation to a new church building. We were involved with the Inuit land developers who had plans to develop a large tract of land, which the church controlled. They were to provide a new church building with access privileges to what was a large shopping development. Several meetings were held with City Hall and certain lawyers. The entire project never materialized but the church ended up with a substantial amount of funds, which were ultimately used in relocation under the leadership of the new Pastor, Rev. Gary Fricker.

We terminated our time with the induction of the new pastor and left with a host of new friendships and a feeling that the Lord had enabled us to make a contribution to God's work at Port Moody. The assembly relocated and is still being a real witness for the Gospel. We were still part of the District Executive as Assistant Superintendent and shared in the administration of our District Fellowship.

Later that year we attended a conference (COPOL) in Toronto, and finished off the year with two weeks in Puerta Vallarta. I should mention that on our first visit to Puerta Vallarta we bought four weeks of timeshare at Villa del Palmar. The family and ourselves have used it many times and when we were unable, we rented it out. Presently it is for sale.

For a period of time at this point in our lives, we were not involved in any specific charge. We attended Broadway Church where our family attended and enjoyed the blessing and ministry of Pastor George Smith and the congregation.

In 1994 a schedule of speaking engagements, e.g. Dunbar, West end, Anugrah and Rock Creek in the Kootenays, kept us busy. We visited Victoria for a weekend, ministered at Port Moody and took a two-week holiday in Hawaii. We spoke at Delta, taught Bible class at Broadway for 4 Sundays and then ministered in Prince George at the Native church, which was a great exciting time with Pastor Larry Jones and the native folk. Their church facility was a former bar and restaurant.

We traveled to Winnipeg for 5 days, then back at Broadway, and spoke at their Senior's retreat at the Firs. We also ministered at Boundary Road Seniors, Broadway Lodge, and Vancouver Native church. We then traveled to Vernon, Calgary, Russell, Winnipeg, Brandon, then back to Calgary, and home. Later, we went to Toronto for General Conference. We were picked up by Don Shantz and spoke Sunday night at Kitchener by the invitation of our friend Ken Bombay.

Shortly after returning home, Grace and I traveled to Winnipeg. We called upon Mike and Lena at Russell and then got an emergency call from my sister Helen who was very ill. We spent a week tending to Helen who was finally admitted to Grace hospital. Cheryl and Charlene flew to Winnipeg to be with Helen and visited her in the hospital, and we returned home. On September 10, the girls phoned us that Helen had passed away.

They were visiting with her, caring for her 'appearance' needs, and having a wonderful time. They left to go to her apartment for a short change, but with plans to return soon. While they were there, the Hospital called to say that Helen had passed away. It seemed that when my sister had this timely visit with Cheryl and Charlene she was ready to make her departure from this life.

We returned to Winnipeg and made all the arrangements for her funeral. Long before her death, Helen made most of the arrangements and pre-paid all costs. She indicated that there would be no need for any extensive service; however, I wanted to have a proper service for her. My friend, Pastor Barber, accepted my request that he officiate at her service. Back in 1971 Pastor Barber took the services when my mother passed away.

There was a lovely service on Sept 13 and a goodly number of people came. Herb did a wonderful job, with a lunch to follow. We buried Helen beside Bill. The girls could not stay for the service, having to return home. But before leaving, they were a great help in the couple of days prior to the funeral service and they wrote a lovely letter of thanks to their aunt for the wonderful memories they had of times spent with her. Immediately following, we had to dismantle the apartment and dispose of everything. As I said, the girls were a vital part of the personal matters.

What remained was disposing of the furnishings, etc. Marion, Sharon and her husband were a great help and Helen had long before indicated what she wanted Sharon to have. Sharon, over a long period of time, had taken a special interest in Helen, doing many things for her and being a real niece to her aunt. We were able to complete all the arrangements with the Wellesly Apartment and other business matters. We then loaded many personal items in the car and returned home to Vancouver.

We finished off the year with a visit from Mike and Lena in October. In December, we took a cruise through the Panama Canal visiting several extremely interesting points. The cruise ended in Aruba. From there, we flew back through Cancun, Mexico to our home in Vancouver.

In 1995 a busy time with adventures and opportunities, never envisioned, came our way. The following are some of our activities which included a decision to accept a church position. In our continuing role as a Board member of Pacific Academy, we attended a retreat in Victoria. We then took a 2-week holiday to Hawaii.

We ministered in Prince George March 31 to April 3. On May 14-21 we went on an Alaska Cruise. Seeing that part of our country was most interesting. It was a fun time with the group, which included our friends Norm and Jean Smith. We ministered at the Vancouver Chinese Church, attended Ken and Helen Roberts 50th anniversary and in August had a very nice visit from Mike and Lena.

# Broadway Church

We already were a part of the Broadway congregation when a member of the Board and Pastor Smith approached us to become part of the pastoral staff and be responsible for the Adult Ministries. In response to their request on August 2, 1995 we submitted a summary of what we envisioned this department to be and our involvement with it. The result was that we were appointed to assume the responsibilities in August 1995.

We proceeded to set up the programs of luncheons, coffee hour, Manor activities, and teaching the Adult Christian Education class. We ministered the Word in the Sunday night sanctuary service on November 12. We had stipulated that we wished to be free to minister elsewhere as we did in White Rock and attend such events as funerals, (Lil LePalm) and a 50th anniversary (Schindels), as well as take pre-planned holidays as we did to Mexico (October 7-21).

It was an honor to participate in this new role as part of the Pastoral Staff with only one area of responsibility. It turned out to be very enjoyable not to have to carry the whole load as a Senior Pastor, as was our past pastoral experience. Pastor George Smith and his wife Barbara were most congenial and made us feel very comfortable. This warm relationship extended to the whole time of Pastor Smith's tenure and afterwards.

Another full year would await us in 1996 with our task at Broadway as well as other external events. The adults of Broadway received us with enthusiasm and love. We set up an executive, and plans were laid for various types of ministries to the adults. It would turn out to be a most fulfilling time for the adults as well as for Grace and me. We hosted events with a good attendance, e.g. monthly luncheons, the Paddle wheeler outing, False Creek cruises, and class teaching plus some 39 calls, visits and counseling. It turned out to be almost a full time ministry.

This was the year or my 45th graduation class reunion held in Vancouver, where as a group, we shared in the morning service in Broadway Church. Our celebration was held in the Sandman Hotel with 12 graduates and their spouses. A number of the graduates could not make it.

Other events were several funerals, the 50th anniversary of Rev and Mrs. John Watts, holidays in June to Hawaii and to Palm Desert in November. General conference was held in Toronto in August with a stop over in Vernon to visit friends.

The hardest event in this year was a visit to my brother Mike in May when he was in Winnipeg Hospital. We had a very nice time together when Lena and Dale had to go to Russell on business. I returned home and then received the news that Mike had passed away. So Grace and I flew back to Russell. We rented a car and drove to Russell for the funeral that was held on May 23. I say this event was hard, as Mike was the last of our immediate family to pass away, which left me as the only survivor. There are still the survivors of Marion (Dan's wife), Margaret (Carl's wife) and Lena (Mike's wife) and their families. When this happened, I was prompted to start on this biography so my own children would know a history of my side of the family and my travels as well.

# 1997

I will relate some highlights of this year, hoping it will be of interest especially to my daughters. They will be able to relate to much of this time but they wouldn't necessarily know all that dad was doing.

In January, we went to Puerto Vallarta, Mexico for a week. February 28-March 3, we went for a visit to Norm and Jean Smith's and later in March had a visit from Mona Franklin and Noreen Shobrooke. In May, we flew to Winnipeg and attended the 90th anniversary of Calvary Temple, our home church. It was a most rewarding time, meeting old friends and really celebrating. It brought back many memories. They had a re-broadcast of the Old Gospel Fireside Hour where Grace played the piano and sang.

After we returned home, in May, Grace had an angiogram of her neck to check for any blockage. In June we had our 50th adult retreat at Heritage Valley with Joe Johnson. This was a great success. At the end of June, there was the farewell service with George Smith. This was the year that Cheryl directed the music at Broadway and she put together a great 'encore' musical. The platform was beautifully decorated and she had me do the narration. It was a great success.

This was the time when Jim Cantelon became the pastor. The pulpit was filled with special speakers and with congregational meetings. Rev. Cantelon was called at the end of August. We took 2 weeks holiday to Hawaii.

The year was completed with Dwyer, Edstrom, Shep, Phillips, Siford, Klassen, Calder, and Spratt funerals, plus luncheons and Bible classes and many calls. Our job at Broadway was to be part time, but turned into a full time ministry. On November 13, we took time to visit Lena who now lived on Salt Spring Island.

## 1998

Another interesting year was in store for us during 1998. We began with 2 weeks of rest and relaxation at Palm Springs, where we stayed at a very nice Spa Resort. Renting a car while there, we visited with Bill and Betty Copeland, and toured the desert countryside. These sightseeing trips were very attention grabbing. While there, as we visited an Indian Reserve, a cactus bit me.

Back home we conducted Marie Weinheimer's memorial service and had eye surgery (cataracts). Officiating at funerals included: H. Magnus, Newberry, Matson. I spoke at rallies in Powell River and Abbotsford. Also, at the Mortgage burning service at Connaught Heights.

April 24 to May 10 we took a cruise traveling to London, in the English Channel, Lisbon, Gibraltar, Malaga, Mediterranean, Cannes, Portofino, Rome and returned to London to take a bus tour with Trafalgar along the east coast of England, Stratford, Edinburgh, Scotland; then back to west side Glasgow, London and home.

The cruise was great and we saw some very interesting country. We passed through Gibraltar at night. Rome Airport was quite a zoo. The England and Scotland bus tour was interesting, Scotland was picturesque.

From July 12 to October 8 we served as interim pastor at Delta. We had a very enjoyable time ministering to this great congregation. We worked with the board and search committee for a pastoral candidate. I appreciated working with Bill Ashbee and Ron McKee. We filled in this year appointment and still carried our duties at Broadway Church.

Back home with our Broadway duties, we had a retreat with Joe Johnson, and conducted a funeral for Richard Beital (only 8 years of age). I dedicated him as a baby at Connaught. Mrs. Blair's funeral. We flew to Saskatoon to attend our 50th class graduation reunion. We had a great time. We and the Lothers drove out afterward to Asquith, my first Pastorate. The old church was turned into a fire hall.

In August we attended the Wuerch and King 50th Wedding anniversary celebrations. It was nice to meet more of Mark's relatives. King's celebration was held at Kevin's home and it was a great time to meet many of the Glad Tidings folk. On September 10 we conducted the memorial service of our old friend Bernard Parkinson at the special request of his son Bob. In September we attended Carleen Hornby's wedding and reception. It was a gala celebration with a large reception. Rob Argue (Carleen's grandfather) shared in the event.

On November 8 we installed Dwight Soleski as the pastor of Delta. Then there were a couple of funerals: Mrs. Krausher who helped us with her son and daughter-in-law at our social functions, and a special service for Mr. Steve Shabak. Brother Steve, the father of Anne Watts was a real friend and a member of our congregation at Connaught Heights. He lived in the Villa next door and we had many pleasant visits with him.

On Wednesdays we spoke at the 10:00 a.m. service in the chapel and almost every Wednesday, Steve wanted us to have lunch with him. Lunch included headcheese, or ham sandwiches with his special cranberry sauce and crusty buns and tea. He often talked about his ministry among the Ukrainian folk in Alberta and Vancouver. He built churches from the logs he took from his farm. Fellowship with him was precious.

Another great event was our honor to officiate at the wedding of Bob Parkinson and Vivian Berry. Bob had become a special friend during our times of counsel and fellowship. The wedding was held at a very quaint historic place in Richmond— the Minoru chapel. It was a delightful time and we have shared nice social times since.

In November, we said farewell to Marjorie Hopper with whom we were associated in Victoria, New Westminster and Vancouver as part of "Another Chance Ministry." Our association with Marjorie, since our first meeting in Victoria to this date, was filled with events and fellowship, which would take a book I do not wish to write at this point.

As I recall, this year was filled with many calls, activities, socials and ministry in Broadway and elsewhere. It was a good year and I am thankful for God's blessing and good health for 50 years of active ministry.

# 1999

This would be the threshold year of Y2K. Another 12 months and we would enter the year 2000. Our journey would continue with no real let-up. We started the year with holidays to Hawaii, January 2-9. This was always a great time with sun and swimming and hiking up to Diamond Head. Cheryl and Charlene were with us, which made for a good time.

Upon returning, I had eye surgery for cataracts and implants. In February, we shared in the service of our close friend Doris Gaffney in Victoria. In March and April we went with the family during Spring break to Puerto Vallarta, Mexico.

Back home, we spoke at a luncheon at Seaview in White Rock. This was another year of funerals. These included Joyce Watts, Gordon McNutt, Chas Hoare, Tom Martin, Sr., Mrs. Winnie Shannon, Sandra Hoeppner, Ernie Frances, Mr. Nomm and Rita McKee.

I might say in regard to Rita, she was in her nineties and had credentials with the Pentecostal Assemblies for 72 years. I was at her bedside when she breathed her last—a beautiful home going. We also attended the 90th anniversary of the

Kitchener Church where we pastored and built a new church.

I spoke at the morning service on May 30 and Monday at an afternoon rally and had to leave for home as Gordon McNutt had passed away and the funeral was on Tuesday, June 1. July 2, we attended a Western Pentecostal Bible College re-union in Abbotsford. August 15 we attended the 50th anniversary of our friends, Bob and Ruby Fleming, in Victoria. On August 27-29 we had our 50-Plus retreat at Heritage Valley with Herb Barber as our guest speaker. It was a real time of blessing and enjoyment for all.

September 3 is a very special date for Grace and me. It was our 50th wedding anniversary. Our girls, Cheryl and Charlene, did a magnificent job in conducting this event. It was held at the Vancouver Golf Club and beautifully decorated with enlarged pictures of us from our young days to the day of our wedding. We had most of our wedding party present. They included Rob Argue (who married us), his wife Mary-Ellen, Dorothy Wright (Carson) bridesmaid, Judy Rogerson ( Argue) our flower girl, and Norman Swanson, my usher.

The only ones missing were my sister Helen (who was deceased), and my best man Vance Carson who was unable to attend. Musical guests included violinist Don Patz, soloist Norm Birch, and pianist Bev Neville. Special people included my cousin Judy Evans (Cloverdale) and my sister-in–law Lena Ostapowich from Salt Spring. Grace's two nieces Brenda and Darlene and their families from Calgary and Surrey attended. Other special friends came from Victoria, Vernon, Kennewick, Washington; Kelowna and Vancouver areas.

Our special thanks went to Ron Booker and Peter Rogerson for making a videotape of the whole event. We all sat down to a beautiful banquet and a most joyous program. As I have said, my girls did a fantastic job of planning this special event. We will not ever forget the warmth of greeting and wishes from everyone.

In October, at Broadway Church, we celebrated the "United Nations the year of older people" with special speaker Robert Taitinger. This included a banquet, a special adult choir and a spiritually-moving Sunday service. This was to honor our older people, and all enjoyed the event.

Immediately after, we took a cruise to Athens, Israel, Suez Canal, Red Sea, Arabia and finally to Bombay, India. We flew back to London and home. It was a most interesting cruise with stops at many places of interest and remarkable countries.

I wish I could describe the various people and places that we saw. It was the history of the Old World, and it would take much time to really discover and digest what that world was like. We were thankful for the brief opportunity we had to travel in that area of the world.

Upon returning home we continued with our duties at Broadway with all the adult activities, Bible classes and speaking at Shiloh—one of the Broadway's seniors complex. On December 18, we cruised on Jim Pattison's yacht, which participated in a Christmas Lights tour.

How blessed we were to have this fun time, as I understand the Pattison vessel would no longer participate in future events. All told, I counted up some 110 events for this year. I'm supposed to be semi-retired. Oh well, I loved it!

# 2000

This year began with a pastoral change. Jim Cantelon resigned. The staff had a farewell supper at the Laterratza, Pacific and Cambie. We continued with our Broadway ministry of visitation. One time we went to visit Bill Goodall in the West end. Coming to the apartment door, we suspected that with no answer something was wrong. I walked away and felt I should contact the police. Just then a cruiser with two Vancouver policemen drove by and I hailed them down and indicated who I was and of my suspicion. They immediately checked and forced the door open to find Bill dead on the floor like I saw when looking through the window.

An ambulance was summoned. We stayed to observe the process of the removal of the body. It was later ascertained that he had been dead for two days. I indicated to the policeman my readiness to serve on behalf of the church. Ultimately we had the service in consultation with the officials of Vancouver City where Bill worked, as well as the railway museum where Bill was an active member.

Since he had no family connections, except for being part of my Sunday school class and his Pastor, we arranged a service with a member of the Vancouver City who was a close friend. The service was held in Broadway's Chapel on February 18, 2000.

Later when we were dismantling his apartment, Vancouver City executives asked that the church take all of Bill's books. He was a prolific reader and all the materials were Christian studies and reference books on the Scriptures. Some of the pastors took whatever books they desired.

Many of the mementos of Bill's interest in the railway are today displayed in the Vancouver Museum. The balance of funds were donated to Broadway church. It's quite remarkable what a pastor gets involved with, but it was an honor for me to be able to serve in this service in honor of Bill Goodal.

While I'm on the subject of funerals, this year was one in which we conducted the funeral and memorial services of some very prominent people. I will highlight them with a brief comment. Some were great servants in ministry with whom we had fellowship. There was Gordon Hardy, the quartet singer. Gordon served in our churches in Alberta and B.C. as a dedicated layman. Another outstanding minister was Rev. John Watts whose missionary service and pastoral posts at Calgary and Broadway church were highly acclaimed. Then there was Mrs. Elsie Blundell, who with her husband, served as pastors and evangelism spanning many years across the USA and Canada. Both Mel and Elsie were artists and we have several of their paintings in our home. Mrs. Blundell, from her large family, had 22 grand children, 45 great grandchildren and 6 great great grandchildren. A remarkable lady.

Another associate with me was Albert Schindel who served in B.C. pastorates with his wife Beth. In September we shared in the memorial service for Beth who for numbers of years endured a stroke condition until her passing. It would be that next year Albert would pass away, which we will mention under the 2002 heading. They were such a great help and blessing to us when we served as pastors at Connaught Heights in New Westminster. We enjoyed a very close friendship with them right up to their departure to be with the Lord.

We were shocked when Gordon Veal suddenly passed away. He was part of my Adult executive, a bass singer with the Choraliers and always ready to help in so many ways as an organizer, carpenter—all this with a lovely Christian spirit. We will remember the great crowd that gathered for his memorial service on May 15, 2000. There were other Broadway people like Mrs. English, Betty Harrison, Mrs. Moyseyeck, Mr. Knudson, on whose behalf we ministered to the families in their time of loss.

This year was filled with many activities, special hymn singing events, speaking at Broadway's morning services during pastoral change, luncheons and baby dedications.

We were able to take holidays in Maui and at Harrison, where we purchased our Park trailer. We also went to the Okanagan to visit friends; to Salt Spring to see family; and also to Mexico. It was a good year to give thanks to God for the blessings of health and all the friends with whom we shared lasting fellowship and memories.

# 2001

This year was filled with various activities. We were still on staff at Broadway carrying for those who passed away. These were Roy Bardock, Mr. Ruthven, Eileen Smith (Dahlberg), Albert Schindel (to whom we referred in year 2000), Mr. Fuller, Martha Winters and Glen Thome.

I note so many funerals because it was a privilege to serve families in their time of bereavement. Many of these deceased were more than just persons with whom we enjoyed a close friendship. It was for me a very rewarding privilege to provide pastoral care, which transcended ministerial duties. I have been commended many times by these people as to the comfort and the inspired hope of the resurrection message that I gave to them.

Over the many years of pastoral ministry to congregations with a number of elderly folk, our personal fulfillment over the hundreds, which we served, is that we were able to convey a message of eternal hope.

In this year, after 20 years (1980) since my heart surgery in Victoria, I had to have an angioplasty. A surgical stent procedure was performed. This is a catheter-based procedure in which a small, expandable wire mesh tube (stent) is inserted into an artery as a scaffold to hold it open. This was performed to clear my two-decade old by-pass procedure. I understand according to my doctors that I am quite a miracle to go that long after open-heart surgery. For this we give thanks to God.

For a period of time we served as interim pastor at Central Assembly, giving counsel and ministering to that congregation. In May, we attended the 75th anniversary in Brandon, Manitoba where we pastored for many years.

We accepted several speaking engagements at Connaught, Chilliwack and Abbotsford. We took a leave of absence for a couple of months during the summer. We got together with old friends Paul and Velo Barber, Lionel and Audrey Brathwaite, Mr. & Mrs. Gordon Allan, and our Okanagan friends.

A highlight for the year was when in August and September we went on a Baltic Cruise visiting London, Norway, Sweden, Finland, St. Petersburg, Russia; Talin and Copenhagen. It was a real education to visit these countries and obtain a historical view of the uniqueness of each of these places and their people. We wouldn't have missed these trips, which have given to us a little bird's eye view of those parts of the world.

A very interesting part of this visit was to be in St. Petersburg, Russia. You felt like walking through history, seeing the various cathedrals, museums and castles of the old royal family heads of state. The city was very picturesque with the canals and statues of government leaders.

Kent Eby, a native of Pennsylvania who had been in Russia for some nine years and spoke fluent Russian, led the tour. He was the director of the established Christian University of St. Petersburg. He gave us the history of the construction of the excellent campus. Apparently he had difficulty in getting a building permit from city hall because the lady in charge, being a strong communist, opposed the establishment of this institution.

The story goes like this. Ken and his board proceeded with the construction and had faith that God would work things out. A beautiful building was completed and housed all the required needs for the 69 students who attended. All the students were men who came from various countries in that part of Europe.

These were outstanding young men, training to go back to their countries and establish the Gospel witness and build churches. They were there with deep Christian convictions and had to really study. They were required not only to be able to speak their own language, but had to learn to speak and write Greek and Hebrew. We enjoyed a time of lunch and fellowship with these most outstanding young men.

I mentioned the erection of the facility including plans to renovate and complete an adjacent building for additional accommodations, plus a chapel. Having the first phase constructed, which was first class, they wanted to have the official opening and dedication. Up to now they still didn't have the permit to build, let alone for occupancy.

Kent was able to establish a close and friendly relationship with the Governor of the area. He invited him to attend the opening and cut the ribbon. The event went off without a hitch and got extensive coverage in the local papers. When the lady who had held up the necessary permits found out what had happened and knowing who officiated at the opening, she immediately issued the permit because it could have jeopardized her job.

The University board rejoiced that God had overseen the whole enterprise and honored the faith to proceed. We rejoiced with them and when we left to return to the ship, we prayed for God's blessing upon Kent, his wife, and the entire University and staff and its future. Other activities for this year included time at our Harrison trailer, and fellowship with Paul Barber. We shared lunch and fellowship with Rev. & Mrs. Gordon Allan, with whom we had previous associations. Gordon was 91 years of age and sharp as a tack. Two trips included a time at Whistler and a couple of weeks in Las Vegas, which is quite a city. We didn't play the slots nor did we win.

Throughout this autobiography we made mention of a number of tours and cruises we were able to take. I wish to especially acknowledge that these were made possible by the complete travel arrangements and scheduling made by Myrtle Olson and her husband Mel.

All in all it was a good year with many interesting and enjoyable events. At the same time, we continued with our responsibilities at Broadway, having appreciated the leave of absence during the summer time.

# 2002

Another year of activities and ministry as a part time pastor of Adult and Pastoral Care Ministries, together with personal requests from our host of acquaintances. Funerals included Emily Olson, Ken Cox, Viola Smith, Margaret Sawatsky, Elizabeth Wong (Charlene's friend), Erica Guildemeister; also there was the Kulak baby dedication, and wedding of Cynthia Martin.

Also included were: the 60th anniversary of Jim and Mable Davis; the 50th anniversary of Dr. & Mrs. Islie; the 50th anniversary of Andy and Leah Hagen; the 50th anniversary of Ken and Grace Walker for whom we officiated at a renewal of their vows. And last but not least, the 50th anniversary of Tom and Val Ranson in Kelowna.

On February 20 Grace received her 50th year certificate from the Pentecostal Assemblies of Canada. This year we also tendered our resignation from being on staff at Broadway church after serving in this capacity for seven years. This took place on May 20. Immediately thereafter we went as the speaker to the Okanagan Senior Camp where I ministered eight times and renewed fellowship with many friends in that area.

Upon returning we were asked to fill in as interim pastors at Connaught Heights where we previously served. We enjoyed being back, had great services, engaged special music and shared with the Board in their search for a new pastor. We also ministered at Seaview Seniors luncheon, and at

the Boundary Road Christmas eve service, with two inter-
preters—one Chinese and the other Iranian.

During spring break we traveled with Mark, Charlene
and Aaron to the Dominican Republic. Then, right after our
time at Connaught we enjoyed vacationing in Hawaii for a
couple of weeks.

In September I had an angiogram, followed by an
angioplasty in December. Also in September Broadway had a
special luncheon in recognition of our years on the staff. It is
so nice to have so many friends where we shared in banquets
at the churches as well as in homes. These were times of rich
fellowship with people to whom we ministered in various
ways. At a time when we were completing 54 years of public
ministry, it was very fulfilling for Grace and me.

# Post 2002

During the next years we enjoyed many activities both
personal and various type of ministry. We are told that one
never really retires from Gospel Ministry. For several
Sunday's we taught the adult Bible study at Broadway, conducted special business meetings and spoke at Coquitlam
Christian Centre for my friend Garry Fricker.

There were funerals of Diane Thompson in Connaught,
Dela Elving from Broadway, Weldon Jones in White Rock,
John Tompson in Connaught, Jamie Kubryn in Summer-
land, Garless Milley, Winnie Taguchi, Vancouver; Florence
Krause, Fort Langley; Dave Webber, Vancouver.

We ministered in Connaught Heights, Parkdale Home,
Seten Village, Broadway Lodge, Morgan Creek, Phillipino
session, Surrey Seniors and Langley Gospel church. There
was the 60th anniversary for Les and June Symons, 60th anniversary for John and Ella McBride and 50th anniversary
for Gerald and Ruth Morrison in West Bank, B.C. Just prior,
we enjoyed some time visiting with Norm and Jean Smith in
Vernon and the Ransons in Kelowna. It was also a beautiful
time with the family and different friends.

Holidays included Whistler and an October cruise from
Fort Lauderdale to Moon Cay, St. Thomas, Martinique, Trin-
idad, Margarita, Caruso (Venezula) in the eastern Carribean,

and of course brief times at our Harrison trailer. Grace also went to Brandon for a few days, and enjoyed a wonderful visit with our friends there.

Into 2004 we went to Puerta Vallarta for 2 weeks. We just got back and had to conduct the funeral for our friend George Beitel. Later, we conducted the funeral for our great missionary, Florence Spence. Further services were for Don Taylor and June Symons from Broadway, and Louise Hemelop and Ken Quackenbush from Connaught.

We also conducted a grave side service in Chilliwack for Mr. Martin, father of our friend Donna Sawchenko. We shared in the anniversary of Connaught Heights in April and have been asked to minister on a number of occasions in this church by Pastor Dan Eagle.

It was also a special privilege to conduct the funeral and memorial service for our friend Doll Conway—a long-standing member of Broadway. We conducted the funeral service for my fellow college associate Donald Patz in Ferndale, Washington in August of 2004. More funerals conducted for John Eden and Eva Wolf who were members of Connaught Heights Assembly while I pastored there. It seems we never stop with funeral services. We officiated at the service for Mr. Fred Letvinshuck (Susan Collins father) and shared in the service for Annie McQuat in Chilliwack, who was a long time friend of the family during Saskatchewan days.

We took three weeks in September for holidays at Waikii Beach in Honolulu, Hawaii with excellent weather, staying at our Ohana membership hotel. Our annual Brandon get together was held at Audrey and Lionel Brathwaithe's home. It is always a joy to share with retired ministers and friends and former members of those we pastored. It was a special honor to visit with my friend Harold Pendray for over a year. He was laid up with poor health, during which time we were able to assist him in attending to some of his affairs.

As we conclude this year with my precious family Grace, Cheryl, Charlene, Mark and grandson Aaron, I give thanks to God for good health and leave the future in God's sovereign will. As the Lord provides continued health and strength we will probably continue to serve and minister to many lives as the need arises.

# Chapter 7

## *Thanksgiving Tribute*

I have written extensively about my travels and activities to this point in my biography. The intention was not to boast in any way, but a desire to make a record what has been for God's glory and not of myself.

I look back with amazement at what I was privileged to be as a servant of the Lord. It could be summed up in the title, 'A Mere Farm Boy' protected and guided by God's almighty hand. But I want to record here that I was not alone in my travelogue life.

I wish to pay special tribute and gratitude for the love of my life, my wife Grace. Without her outstanding contribution to my ministry, I could never have accomplished much in myself alone. I am stating the fact that she has been the best pastor's wife a man could have. Words are inadequate to describe what a helpmate Grace has been to my entire family and me. She has always been a beautiful and loving wife and an outstanding mother to our daughters. She has tremendous culinary gifting, an excellent cook, a beautiful hostess and entertainer. Our home was always in order and spotless.

Members of all our congregations acclaimed her as the most remarkable pastor's wife. She shared in every aspect of the ministry. Her musical talents were superb as a pianist and choir director, Sunday school and Kid's Choir leader and teacher. She was a spiritual counselor to members of the congregation in her visitations. She made these calls on her own while the girls were in school but was always home for their arrival from school. They would come home and open the door and shout 'Hi Mom' and were never disappointed to not hear, 'I'm here', 'How was school?', 'Did you have a good day?' and 'What did you learn today?'

Then it was time to give early piano lessons and then later to take them to Brandon University for more advanced lessons. Grace shared in the load of pastoral ministry taking every opportunity to support my concerns, plans, projects and burdens of being a pastor. Her counsel and encouragement was always so valuable and insightful. She had a special intuition and discerning gift, like her mother, which were such valuable assets to know that our plans were directed under the additional guidance of the Holy Spirit.

When I was involved in executive and ministerial activities and away from my charge, she held the post with loving distinction. The congregations loved her and never was she an offence to anyone in dress and work. Her deportment and spirit blessed the people and helped make my ministry what it was. We were in every sense a team and the congregations became the beneficiary of our leadership. The church always said they hired me but they got two for the price of one.

I also want to acknowledge our two daughters, Cheryl and Charlene. It is not easy to be a Preacher's Kid (PK). They were always watched and often judged by the friends they had in the church, school and community. Sometimes they were hurt by being excluded when they would say 'Don't tell her, she'll tell her Dad or Mom,' especially if it was something they should not be doing or saying. Both girls made a personal decision to accept the Lord without any coercion and they used their talents in the church services. They always did well in school and have completed university education and degrees in Counseling and Nursing.

Although I was a bit of a workaholic and always available to my congregation, we as a family took holidays and shared in travels across the country, to the cottage, with our trailer and had lots of fun together.

Today I am the proud father of two Christian girls and still share our time together with the beautiful addition of Mark our son-in-law and Aaron our grandson.

As I look back on my life from its beginning as a little known farm boy in a small Manitoba town and moving on to complete high school, Business college, Navy Career and Bible College and then to fifty-seven years of varied Gospel ministries, I say thanks be to God.

During this lifetime we have seen many wonderful things, met scores of wonderful people and observed continuous changes. Our world has experienced more discoveries, inventions, and advances in the last seventy-five years than in any previous period in history. We are living in a technical world that has made our planet a small ball.

Considering my ancestry, I have been the recipient of all the good that has come with the changes which previous generations never enjoyed. One could ask how prior generations would react if they saw and heard how people perform today and what they enjoy. From my observations of these decades, one cannot help but ask whether society would be better off without some of the changes that mankind calls "progress".

With all the material benefits and technical facilities, the spirit of unrest, aggression and unspiritual attitude is revealed in humanity. No doubt, many of the undesirable and destructive problems we face today are the result of an unthankful and unholy generation.

My prayer has always been and will continue to be that all in our contemporary society will conduct themselves on the basis of a return to a faith of our fathers, which was anchored to a fear of God and the keeping of His Commandments. It is tragic that society has every kind of a solution but will not try the only solution, i.e. the true Christian Faith as defined in the Holy Scriptures.

Although I am no longer in pastoral ministry, I still have opportunity to serve when occasioned by invitations from time to time. Even though in Gospel circles, the changes that have taken place and are dominant in worship today are unlike the kind of ministry, which characterized traditional form, we must seek the unity of the Spirit in the bond of peace.

My prayer is that the church will remain true to the preaching of the Word, and be attendant to the clear connection between prayer and manifestation of the Holy Spirit's power. If these do not remain as our Christian resolve, I fear that the main thrust of the Gospel witness will no longer be center-stage in the ministry of the Church to a lost and dying world!

These basics are what will empower the church to meet the desperate need of humans today. May the body of Christ arise in the power of the Gospel and move with objective conviction by the power of the Spirit of God!

I would like to conclude my story with the words of a hymn so loved by remarkable missionary, Rev. J.R. Spence:

### "The Last Mile of the Way"
**by Benson,Oatman and Marks**

*If I walk in the pathway of duty*
*If I work to the close of the day*
*I shall see the great King in His beauty*
*When I've gone the last mile of the way.*

*And if here I have earnestly striven*
*And have tried all His will to obey*
*'Twill enhance all the rapture of heaven*
*When I've gone the last mile of the way.*

*When I've gone the last mile of the way*
*I will rest at the close of the day*
*And I know there are joys that await me*
*When I've gone the last mile of the way.*